Author's no

I was born in Dunfermline on a Thursday, in March 1937. The rhyme, *Thursday's Child Had Far to Go*, turned out to be true for me. As a child, when I met a missionary at a Junior Christian Endeavour meeting in Viewfield Baptist Church, I was all set to go back with her to India. Twenty-two years later, I did go to India and was there from 1966 to 1999.

I grew up in Canmore Street Congregational Church, Dunfermline (later United Reformed Church), attending the Sunday School and Youth Fellowship and became a church member. I was a girl guide in St Leonard's Church of Scotland.

After a commercial course at school, working in the Youth Employment Service for 10 years and spending three years in missionary training under the London Missionary Society at Carey Hall in Selly Oak, Birmingham, I set sail for India. After language study in Bangalore, I served in the Rayalaseema Diocese, Andhra Pradesh.

I met Leslie Robinson in Edinburgh before he went to India in 1962, as a medical missionary, then again in Bangalore when I was in the Language School and over the years at our annual gathering of missionaries. In January 1979, we were married in Gooty, in Andhra Pradesh, where I had first lived. Leslie was by now a general surgeon and Medical Superintendent of CSI Hospital, Chickballapur, Karnataka. I served with him there, until we retired to Rutherglen in 1999. I discovered that Leslie was also born on a Thursday. In October 1996, Leslie received the OBE from the Queen. This was 'for medical services to the Commonwealth in South India'. Sadly, Leslie passed away in February 2017.

I typed annual letters and sent them by airmail, to my friend Grace Dunlop. I realised that for most of my time in India there were no email facilities available and that my letters to her were sent by airmail. She retyped them and sent them out to friends. The number of recipients grew as over the years, people in the UK supported our work in India.

– Betty Robinson (nee Williamson)

Dedicated to all my missionary colleagues, and Indian friends.

Betty Robinson

THURSDAY'S CHILD HAD FAR TO GO

From Scotland to India

To Lynda
Best wishes!
From Betty Robinson

AUSTIN MACAULEY PUBLISHERS™

LONDON • CAMBRIDGE • NEW YORK • SHARJAH

A CIP catalogue record for this title is available from the British Library.

ISBN 9781398430136 (Paperback)
ISBN 9781398431812 (ePub e-book)

www.austinmacauley.com

First Published 2022
Austin Macauley Publishers Ltd®
1 Canada Square
Canary Wharf
London
E14 5AA

I am greatly indebted to my friend, Grace W. Dunlop, a member of Canmore Street Congregational Church, Dunfermline, my hometown and church. Grace retyped and often illustrated the annual circular letters I sent to her by email from India and sent them to friends and family around the world who supported the work.

She carefully preserved the original letters and presented me with the file when she entered a Care Home. Sadly, she passed away in March 2020 so did not see the letters emerge into a book.

After editing the letters, I passed the collection onto friends who encouraged me to have them printed so that the present generation may know of the work of missionaries in India in the last century.

Table of Contents

Council for World Mission—formerly, London Missionary Society.

In 1966, when I sailed to India as a long-term missionary, it was for an initial period of five years. This was followed by a one-year furlough during which there was a period of holiday, the opportunity for further study or training and several periods of deputation throughout the UK arranged by C.W.M. as well as any talks arranged privately. These were to let the local churches know about the work overseas.

When we changed to air travel, this was eventually changed to a system of two years' service followed by four months leave, which included two months deputation work.

Letter 1
Travel to India and First Impressions

Gooty, Andhra Pradesh
South India
4 November 1966

Dear Friends,

It is now two months since I left home to go to India. I am grateful to all who sent good wishes on my departure or who have written to me here.

I was one among a party of six adults and three children who journeyed across the continent and holidayed in Italy before sailing from Venice. We had a wonderful time visiting some of the sights in several towns. Each place we stayed at had a charm of its own. We arrived in Florence in time to see the Lantern Festival. In the afternoon, there were demonstrations of marching, flag-waving and crossbow firing, and in the evening, flares lit the Vichy Palace, and the banks of the river were hung with lanterns. Crowds of people flocked the streets, and many, especially the children, carried long canes with fancy candle-lit paper lanterns. There was a very colourful parade of floats and people in historical costumes. Rome, I shall remember for the wonderful welcome we had from the Sisters of Bethany, in the Foyer Unitas of Piazza Navona. This Roman Catholic Order of nuns provides information on and conducted tours of Rome. The accommodation and amenities provided in the house were first class.

In Rome itself, I was amazed how the old and the new buildings (many centuries apart) mingled happily. It was like taking a step back into history as we walked past the Forum and Coliseum. Leaving this great city, we visited the Pope's summer residence at Castel Gandolfo. Along with many others assembled below his window, the Pope blessed us. Of all the places we stayed at, Assisi was the most charming with the sandy-coloured houses leaning on each other as they stretched up the hillside. It was a joy to walk down the narrow streets with staircases and alleyways and window boxes filled with geraniums and other brightly coloured flowers. The Roman Catholic Centre La Citadella Cristina was our home for one night, and we were well-catered for and welcomed there. The shops were full of carved models of St Francis with his birds and animals, or articles adorned with Assisi embroidery. Certainly, a place I would like to return to. Apart from the churches with their wonderful mosaics, I much preferred the journey to and from Ravenna rather than the town itself.

Travelling was quite an adventure in itself. Luggage featured a lot in our escapades as we had quite a pile amongst us. It was quite a sight to see the assortment of cases, bags, baskets and bundles piled up on a station platform. The operation to transfer all these goods and chattels on to the train and vice versa proved quite entertaining to fellow travellers! We were soon expert at doing our own portering—passing luggage through the train windows, then piling the pushchairs high while the children walked or were carried. Try to imagine getting 25 pieces of luggage and 9 persons into an already-packed train, which arrived late and was preparing to leave in a few minutes! Such was our experience in Florence as we headed for Rome. From Rome onwards, we had arranged to hire a Volkswagen minibus, and this proved much more convenient and comfortable—even though the rear window was completely blocked by luggage! Travelling this way, we were able to stop at leisure for picnics and swims on the route. In some places, very little English was spoken, but Woolworth's Italian phrasebook proved very useful, and it was surprising how well we managed to find our way around, even to shopping for food in the markets. Because of the restrictions about taking money abroad, I understand a bank in England advertises, 'Borrow a baby and see the world'. A baby was certainly the passport to happiness in Italy, as everywhere men and women alike were wreathed in smiles as they stopped to speak to the children. I was glad there were children in our party to share in our adventures. We went on to Venice with its famous waterways and canals. It seems hard to imagine this beautiful city suffering from floods in recent days, and many of its famous works of art damaged. In all the ten days in Italy, it was only as we left Venice that we had our first shower of rain—and even this was not long-lasting.

On my short sea trips to Shetland and Fair Isle or even on occasions crossing the River Forth in the ferry, I have not proved myself a good sailor. The much longer trip from Venice to Bombay (almost 4,000 miles and 16 days at sea) made me a bit apprehensive. However, I did not need to worry as the sea was as calm as could be and hardly a roll was felt the entire journey. As I lazed about on deck in the blazing sunshine, after cooling off in the swimming pool, or worked my way through the menus, I could see why doctors recommend a Mediterranean cruise to build up their patients! It was interesting to stop at various ports on the way.

While the ship went through the Suez Canal, I joined the bus party from Port Said to Suez, visiting the pyramids and various sites in Cairo, including the famous Egyptian museum housing the treasures of Tutankhamen tombs. We had only a short stop at Aden but time to make some purchases in the duty-free shops. There was an uneasy tension in the air as we walked about the streets, with armed soldiers at every corner and jeeps unloading more armed soldiers as we moved along. At one corner, we were warned to go no further by an armed soldier with a broad Glasgow accent! It was grand to hear another Scots accent! As we left the port, there was some trouble with a buoy's cables, which got twisted around our ship's propeller. Frogmen came into operation, and it was several hours before we were able to chug slowly away. After straightening up again (we had listed quite considerably with all the work going on at one side), we were soon back to our normal speed once more.

A short trip by taxi through Karachi left me with the impression of noise, bustle and smell! Cars and buses jostled with pedestrians, stray animals—cats, dogs, cows, sheep and goats—and transport pulled by camels, donkeys and men.

My first view of Bombay's skyline seemed most welcoming. Here, I was, at last, arriving in India after all these years of waiting and preparation. People say, "Every end has a new beginning," and so as one set of adventures and experiences ended, new ones were waiting to take their place. Instead of being right in the harbour, because of a pilots' strike, our ship was about a mile out, and passengers had to leave with hand luggage only, a few at a time, by motorboat. We waited in the customs shed most of the day, expecting our heavy luggage to join us, but we had to abandon this possibility eventually and head for the evening train to Madras.

I travelled with Dora Smith and Alan Cranmer all night and most of the next day, then had to part as we went our separate ways. Eileen Bending, an English LMS missionary, came on the train at Adoni and travelled with me to Gooty, where Pat Roberts, an Australian LMS missionary, was waiting to welcome me to share my first home in India with her.

I met many of the church folk at the Sunday morning service, and although I could not understand what was being said in Telugu, the local language, I enjoyed hearing the Indian lyric tunes. Pat had kindly arranged to leave me free for the first few days in order to unpack trunks and generally settle down, but having no trunks to unpack (they eventually reached me on 26 October) and eager to start learning Telugu, I began on my own, writing the alphabet. When the local assistant pastor, Rev. G.T. Abraham called at the house and volunteered his assistance, I put my tape recorder into use and practised the sounds. With the aid of the recorder, I have been able to learn the Lord's Prayer and some lyric verses in Telugu already.

After a week, I began touring various parts of the diocese, visiting hospitals, schools and mission compounds. Everywhere, there was a welcome—and often a beautiful sweet-smelling garland of flowers—from the Indians and missionaries of all nationalities—Danish, American, Australian and English. One of my first duties as the 'new missionary' was to cut the ribbon at the opening ceremony of a pastor's new house in the village of Pathur. After leading the way into the new parsonage, we were all invited to a meal. Sitting cross-legged on the floor, we were served with curry and rice on leaf plates, eating with our fingers. On another occasion, I was able to join the Bible Women from various parts of the diocese as they met for their annual summer school in Bellary. Before the study part of the course, we had an excursion to Hampe, the famous ancient ruined Hindu city in Mysore state. There were wonderful carvings on the buildings and huge stone sculptures still standing in spite of the destruction by Muslims in the eighteenth century. We went on to visit the new large electric power station at the Tungabhadra Dam.

Travelling from place to place by train, bus, jutka (horse-drawn two-wheeled cart) and cycle rickshaw is quite an adventure. I am slowly learning patience as I wait for hours on station platforms for trains to arrive or crawl through the narrow streets in towns and villages as the bus dodges cows and buffaloes that wander aimlessly along. Trains are even more uncertain than ever just now because of the flooding in the Madras area and the unrest in Andhra Pradesh. A great deal of destruction is being done, especially to railway property as people, mostly college students, are drawing attention to their demand for the fifth steel plant to be built in this state. I am finding it difficult to understand the value of such actions for this is surely hindering rather than helping the country. Many strikes that disrupted Britain were equally hard to understand or tolerate.

In spite of the poverty in a great many places, there is still a smile and a twinkle in the eyes and flowers in the women's hair, to brighten the gloom. The children are especially appealing, even the poorest with their tousled hair and ragged or non-existent clothes. In many places, small boys are dressed as girls, with long hair tied up with ribbons and decked with flowers, to waylay the Evil Eye, which they superstitiously believe will fall upon them. I am still amazed at the number of girlish-looking faces with boys' bare bottoms! In spite of so many children about, I have not seen a single pram. These are superfluous when an older child (in many cases not much older!) can carry his brother or sister around on his hip!

There is so much more I could say about my impressions of new things—food, insects, climate and countryside—but this will keep for another time. I go to the Language School in Bangalore on 18 November and will be there (apart from a short break at Christmas) until April. During this time, the church will decide to which part of the Rayalaseema Diocese it wants me to go.

By the time this reaches you, Christmas preparations will be well underway. Although so far I have seen no signs of tinsel and glitter, or all the usual yuletide fare, I feel the Spirit of Christmas as we sit out of doors in the evenings and look up into the starry sky. I think of the shepherds out on the hillsides with their flocks (those I have seen here are so like Biblical pictures of Palestinian scenes) and the white or sandy-coloured buildings with flat roofs and outside staircase and the donkeys carrying loads along the rocky paths. It is not a far stretch of the imagination to move from an Indian scene (with a mother bending over her tiny baby as it swings in a hammock at the side of her low wooden bed, watched by the cattle and the donkey), to the manger scene in Bethlehem.

As I spend my first Christmas in India, although so far away from you all, we will be united in spirit as we celebrate this Christmas Season together.

Betty

Letter 2
Telugu Language Study in Bangalore

United Theological College
Language Department Hostel
Bangalore
5 March 1967

Dear Friends,

Many thanks to all who have written, sent magazines and Christmas cards—some of which I was still receiving up until the end of February. It helped make Christmas last all the longer! I enjoyed hearing from you all, and thank you for keeping me up to date with the news.

I had a wonderful time at Christmas in Gooty with Pat Roberts and the Marsden family. It was almost like being at home, with children around, especially as they are about the same ages as Fiona and Heather, my nieces. On Christmas morning, carol singers who had been going the rounds of houses since midnight awakened us. At 8 am, the church was overflowing. People were squashed up on the benches, and the floor was packed solid at the front. It was quite a sight to see hundreds of pairs of sandals lined up outside the door. As is usual in an Indian church service, people kept arriving all the way through, and by the end, every inch of space was filled, and others had to stand and look through the open doors and windows. The church was lavishly decorated with paper chains that rustled noisily in the breeze and added to the noise of the children above which the preacher had to make himself heard!

As this is the cooler season of the year, this is the time for sports, and a tennis tournament was held during Christmas week with top players coming from quite far afield to compete. The church also organised a sports day on Wednesday, and I was asked to present the prizes and assist Father Christmas to give presents to the Sunday School children from the Christmas tree.

At Hogmanay, we gave a party in Pat's house for the young people of the church. Indians of all ages like playing games, and we had quite a riotous time as everyone entered fully into all the activities. The time passed quickly, and all too soon, it was time to go to the church for the midnight service. On New Year's Day, at the church service, eight babies and children (including Christopher Marsden) were baptised, and the church was again well filled. I was invited to two homes to share in the baptismal feasts given by the families to celebrate the occasion.

Back in Bangalore, I attended another baptismal service when nine adults received believers' baptism in the open-air baptistery on the church grounds. It was very impressive to be in the congregation standing in a circle around the baptistery hearing the people give their responses and promises. I go regularly to this church, which is for Telugu-speaking people in the area. The church is well filled every Sunday, and I enjoy joining in the lyrics and hymns, though I still don't understand much of the sermon apart from an odd word here and there! The service is entirely in Telugu, but we are advised to go in order to get used to listening to the language we are learning.

A few weeks ago, we were invited to the dedication of one of the church members' new bungalow. After a tour of the very modern house, we had a short service, followed by coffee, curry puffs and cake. (It was quite appropriate, as in the Bible stories, I have been learning in Telugu, the people at the end 'eat, drink and rejoice'. The sermon for that day was about rejoicing, and now, we were completing the Indian custom—eating and drinking!)

On Friday, 10 February, I joined in the service of worship at St Mark's Cathedral, Bangalore, for the Women's World Day of Prayer. As Bangalore is quite a cosmopolitan city, women of all nationalities took part in this service, and it was most impressive worshipping with so many women in this beautiful domed church, knowing that women throughout the world would be sharing in the same order of service.

Now for a bit more about Bangalore. As it says in one guidebook: "Bangalore is not really India—because of the climate, people, buildings etc." Situated 3,000 ft. up, it does not have much extremes of climate that some parts of India have, though it is quite hot enough at times even though this is still winter.

My most important task since November has been learning the Telugu language, and on 9 February (halfway through the intensive course), we had a progress test. This consisted of 1½-hour-long oral part with general conversation, telling stories, reading from the Bible and unseen passages from a reading book, dictation and answering questions on everyday events. A two-hour written paper followed this. My teacher was pleased with the results, and this has given me encouragement for the first-year examinations in mid-April. After going all out for this test, some of us relaxed afterwards at the film *My Fair Lady* being shown in one of the modern cinemas in Bangalore. Various aspects of the film struck me as very appropriate for the time and place. As Eliza Doolittle was struggling with her vowels etc., I saw myself struggling with the new Telugu sounds! Some of the London street scenes of those days could be compared with some Indian scenes today, especially, the market stands and flower sellers. Someone has said that just as England had to see her way through these dark days and improve the social conditions etc. so India is at present still finding her way through this stage. Just as Eliza Doolittle was considered a 'cabbage' and 'so commonly low' by Prof. Higgins, so are some of the poorer Indians treated by their richer neighbours. In one way, Bangalore is a kaleidoscope of contrasts—the rich sailing past in their chauffeur-driven cars, while the poor and the lame hobble along in the gutter; the modern flat-roofed brightly painted houses and the hovels of mud and straw over the wall; the impressive silk saris and the ragged tatters.

The United Theological College is set amid beautiful grounds with the Department of Indian Languages in a block on its own. The two-storeyed building is L-shaped with the school (eight classrooms) and a dining room at one end and single bedrooms and flats for families along the other side. At present, there are eleven students (Helga Olesson from Denmark joining us at mid-term for a refresher course after a short time in St Andrews Hall in Selly Oak, Birmingham; five students are studying for their second-year examinations and five of us are beginning. I am the only new person studying Telugu, and Dora is the only Tamil student, so we rejoice in individual tuition three hours a day.

As the Indian Language Department is a part of the United Theological College, we share in some of the activities with the theological students. Every morning at 7 am in the college chapel, there is a short devotional service led by students and staff. On alternate Thursday evenings, we have a communion service and a Fellowship group. For the latter, all those living on the compound, students, staff members and families are divided into groups for discussion on a variety of topics, concluding with devotions. These are held in the homes of the members of staff and are on the lines of the Methodist 'class'. On Sunday evenings, a full church service is conducted by a member of staff or visiting preacher, with often an Indian lyric sung by students to the accompaniment of tabla, harmonium and violin.

On the sports side, we also joined in the various college activities. Last week, a sports day was held with various track events carried out in a very professional manner. Prior to this, there was a great fever of activity as various heats were run off, tennis, table tennis and badminton tournaments played, plus basketball, volleyball and football games. I enjoyed taking part in some of these events and, by winning several finals, helped my House to win the cup for the year! Prizes and certificates were presented at the College Day when visitors and college friends came for this occasion and enjoyed tea on the lawn, followed by reports from the various departments of the college.

During January and February, we also shared in three weddings of college servants on the compound. The first wedding was held in Tamil in a nearby C.S.I. Church, but unfortunately, I was unable to attend this, though did go to the reception afterwards in the college hall. The platform was decorated with flowers and greenery, and the bridal couple smothered in garlands, sat on a couch to receive the greetings in word and kind from the guests. After giving our congratulations, we sat down with several hundred others (everyone on the compound plus relations) to enjoy a curry meal. Everything seemed to go well on that day (Saturday), and it was a great tragedy to hear of the sudden death of the bridegroom's sister on Sunday morning. This cast a gloom over the whole compound with the mourners wailing throughout the day and night. This also put a damper on the second wedding to be held on Monday. This reception was cancelled, but some of us attended the ceremony in the Roman Catholic Cathedral. It was interesting to see both the bride and groom with garlands around their necks and bouquets in their hands. The bride, according to Indian custom, looked as solemn as was expected of her! The third wedding was that of one of our servants in the language hostel. His was a Hindu wedding, which was very interesting to watch. While a band made as much noise as possible, the priest conducted the ceremony in Tamil. There was a great deal of symbolism as coconuts, rice, milk and fire were handled, and various things chanted over them. Again, we celebrated with a curry feast prepared by the hostel cook. He later told us that over 600 people had eaten!

A few weeks ago, Dora and I spent a weekend with the Milledge family in Vellore. We saw around the hospital, medical college and the leprosy rehabilitation village started by Dr Paul Brand. We were also invited to a farewell dinner party given by the medical students to members of staff who were leaving. Dr Ida B. Scudder, the niece of the founder of Vellore Hospital, was one of these retiring, and it was wonderful to be able to share in the tributes paid to her.

I was told before I came here, "There is more to language school than language learning." I am enjoying sharing in the various activities, seeing new places, playing with the children, killing cockroaches and ants (which vary in size from the minute to the gigantic) and chasing monkeys.

This term finishes about 20 April when I shall be going back to Gooty. I am joining three other missionaries for a holiday in Kashmir! After several days' journey by bus and train, we are to spend some time on a houseboat in Srinagar and then a few weeks in tents up in the snow-covered mountains. On the way there, we hope to see something of New Delhi and the Taj Mahal by moonlight— more adventure stories in my next letter!

It has not been decided where I will be working in the Rayalaseema Diocese, but it looks as if I may be allowed to come back to language school for another term from June to November to prepare for the second-year exams.

When I last wrote, preparations were in hand for Christmas, and now Easter is not far away. In the local C.S.I. Telugu church, on Good Friday, seven Telugu students or members of staff will be speaking on the Words from the Cross during the three-hour service. We hope to see the sunrise as we join in a communion service at 5 am on Easter Sunday morning.

With palm trees all around and donkeys everywhere—tied up outside houses, grazing and wandering about, carrying bundles and people—it won't be hard to picture Palm Sunday and our Lord riding into Jerusalem, along a dusty sun-baked road, with crowds of curious, questioning bystanders.

Wishing you all the blessings of Easter!
Betty

Letter 3
Travel to Agra, Taj Mahal and Kashmir

Bangalore
8 September 1967

Dear Friends,

Many thanks for all the letters, magazines and parcels, which I have received during the past four months. I enjoy hearing from you all and am grateful to you for remembering me in various ways. When I was on holiday, I sent Kashmir postcards to some, but as the Suez crisis occurred, then I fear some of them may have gone amiss.

In my last letter, I was in the midst of plans for Easter. I attended the three-hour Good Friday service in Telugu and enjoyed the experience but did not get all that was said in the seven 'sermons' on the words from the cross. The service was very well attended, from babies in arms to the old and infirm. If my mind strayed during the service, there was plenty to attract attention—babies asleep in various positions, being fed or being hurriedly removed as puddles appeared on the floor. It always amazes me how contented the children are as they are passed from hand to hand and looked after by various women or older brothers or sisters.

My most impressive experience over Easter was attending the Pascal Candle Service at St Mark's Cathedral in Bangalore. This began at 11:30 pm on Saturday evening and went on until 1 am on Easter Sunday. The service began in darkness with only the flickering of the red light above the altar. The minister walked in with a candle and lit the large Pascal candle from which other smaller candles around the altar were lit. From this one light, the light was then passed around the church as deacons lit the candle at the end of each row, and we in the congregation, in turn, passed it along the pews to our neighbour (in the same way that the Kiss of Peace is passed on the in C.S.I. order for communion service). The church was beautifully decorated with strongly scented lilies and blossoms, and the Easter garden display had a real tree, heavy with blossom, growing in it. After cycling home again through the clear star-lit night, we had a few hours' sleep before rising for the 5 am communion service in our college chapel. The congregation processed round the compound singing an Easter carol to the accompaniment of a piano accordion. The language school students climbed up on the roof (flat one with staircase up) of the hostel where we had a wonderful view of the sun rising over the rooftops.

All too soon, the exams were upon us and the end of term. I am glad to say I passed the first-year language school exam—as did all the students in the three languages studied here. To celebrate the end of term, we went as a group to see the film *The Sound of Music* followed by a Chinese meal when we sampled a variety of dishes. Then we were all off in different directions to our various districts. I had a few days in Gooty (in all the heat 118+) to pack for my adventures in Kashmir.

There were six of us altogether in our party, coming from various parts of India. This was the biggest circular tour I have ever done—going about 3,500 miles from east to west coast and northwards out of India altogether! My first stop was in Madras where I stayed with Mrs Devadasan and her family. It was good to see her again after our time in Selly Oak. Several of us from U.T.C. attended the wedding of David Hall (U.T.C. lecturer and Methodist missionary) and Janet Laister (Methodist missionary in Madras state), which took place in Madras. I also had my first visit to the sea since I arrived in India last September.

Then onto Delhi by air-conditioned third-class express train. This is the way to travel in India I found. It was so pleasant cool and dust-free compared to normal railway carriages. There are no sleepers though the seats tilt backwards at an angle. This is fairly comfortable, though for such as me, what to do with long legs was a problem! After two nights and a day on the train, we arrived at Agra where we spent a night in the station retiring room. This was to be the first of many nights spent in such a room. This was as good as a hotel, with Dunlopillo beds, fans, running water and nearby restaurant facilities. Being on the station meant one had not far to go for one's next connection when travelling by rail. This was a boon when travelling with lots of holiday luggage.

Firstly, we went to the Taj Mahal. This visit was in the afternoon in full sunshine. It was simply breath-taking. It was exactly as it is pictured yet so much more beautiful to see in reality. We returned later to see it in full moonlight. Our holiday had been specially timed to include this! It was more awe-inspiring and exuded such peace and calm. I could have sat for hours just looking at it in the moonlight. Eventually, we had to leave, but after a few hours' sleep, we returned to see it at sunrise. Once more, it showed another side as the dawn broke and the marble reflected the sun's rays. A closer examination of the outside and inside showed the intricate and delicate inlaid marble and the dainty beauty of it all. No model or picture can do justice to the real thing.

Then we were off again by train to Delhi where we spent two days sightseeing and shopping. *Son et Lumiere* in the Red Fort helped to tell the history of Old Delhi, which is separated from New Delhi only by the old wall. To see the Parliamentary buildings, Secretariat and President's house and the long wide drive up through India Gate to them was most impressive. All too soon, we had to catch the train for Pathankot, the end of the Indian railway line. We were on our way to Kashmir.

Now, our transport was by bus and the prospect of a 250-mile drive up through mountains and woods, round zigzag bends, and up and down very steep gradients. On the way, there was a slight delay while one of our group had to clamber onto the roof of the bus to look in her trunk for her passport to show at the Jammu border! This was to be the first of many occasions when we had to produce our passports or sign visitors' books etc. The twisting drive through the mountains was very reminiscent of Scotland. This was a comparison I was to make over and over again during our stay in Kashmir. The mountainside in some places was very steep, and landslides were evident in many places so it was not hard to visualise roadblocks during wintry weather. As we negotiated a series of hairpin bends, we were passed by no less than 206 army lorries. We discovered later that these were on their way to base camps with supplies of stores and ammunition and that this was a daily event. It was a nasty reminder that trouble was not far away from this beautiful tourist land. The thought of how easy it would be to create a roadblock made us realise that in spite of its beauty, this would not be the place to be if any trouble arose. However, for the moment, our thoughts were on our holiday and the beauty of the countryside.

As we came down from the snow-capped, fir-covered mountains into the fertile Kashmir valley, we could see lovely purple and white irises growing everywhere and bright red poppies in the field. Here was our home for the next two weeks. This was a very well-appointed houseboat (with a small annex alongside) on the Dal Lake in Srinagar. Small Gondola-type boats (shikaras) lined up for hire at the lakeside, and these took us and our luggage across to the boat. Later, it took us for sails around the lake, along the backwaters and into the rivers. We were well provided for in the houseboat. The owner arranged and conducted us on tours of papier-mâché, brass and copper, walnut woodcarving and carpet making establishments and to see displays of embroidered shawls and table linen etc. The scenery was breath-taking with the snow-capped mountains nearby. In the distance boats loaded with flowers or vegetables for sale, mingled with the water lilies and floating gardens on the lake.

One day, we set off to visit some of the formal gardens created by the Mughal emperors in the sixteenth and seventeenth centuries. It seemed as if spring and summer had come at once as we admired the daffodils, tulips, crocuses, wallflower, pansies, stock etc. growing in great profusion. Setting off on the return journey in a calm sea with a blue sky overhead, we were soon to experience the Biblical 'sudden storm on Galilee' for without warning a strong wind arose. The sky overhead darkened and within a very short time, we were battling for life against a raging storm. As we headed for the safety and shelter on a small island, the wind tore at our straw-thatched roof and blew it partially off. We were in danger of capsizing the boat as the roof, held on by one corner, dragged us over. Once we removed it and dragged it in the water behind us, things were better. Minute by minute, the storm increased in its fury, and at one point, it looked as if we would be blown past the small island. With the help of other picnickers and boatmen, we were caught and held fast. On the island, we took what shelter we could in one of the 'bus-type' shelters. We held matting up and round the side to keep off the worst of the driving wind. After singing our way through the alphabet to cheer ourselves up and keep warm, the rain and storm stopped as suddenly as they had started. We headed back home on a once again calm lake with blue skies telling us how foolish we had been to worry!

As well as visiting the various craft centres, the craftsmen themselves came in their shikaras to visit us at the houseboat and display the wares they had made during the winter months. The exquisitely embroidered articles, carvings, jewellery etc. were all very tempting. The names of the craftsmen were no less exotic—Butterfly, Suffering Moses, Subhanna the Worst, Village Man, etc.

Srinagar is 5,800 feet above sea level, and one day, we went for a bus ride into the mountains near Gulmarg, which rises to 8,500 feet. We went on horseback for the last 4 miles up through the woods to the snow line. We had a closer view of higher snow-capped peaks beyond. The nearby slopes with fir trees set amidst the snow made us think of a Christmas card setting. All too soon, this part of our holiday was over, and we were off again into the mountains for a camping holiday.

Settled in tents on the third plateau at Pahalgam at 7,200 feet, we had a wonderful view up the valleys, down to rushing torrents and waterfalls. Now, we had a chance to do more walking, hiking and riding. After my first experience of being on horseback, I was keen to get in more practice. I enjoy walking but get breathless climbing, so with the assistance of a sure-footed pony, it was an easy matter on the upward climb. I preferred to walk on the downward trail though as I feared I might go right over the pony's head one of these times!

We had two weeks of scorching sunshine, heavy downpours and freezingly cold nights when we went to bed in several layers and with a hot water bottle. Then it was time for the return journey. This time, we split up, and I returned with Pat Roberts via Bombay. This gave me an opportunity to see some more of this city, after the brief look last year when I arrived in India. It seems hard to believe that it is over a year ago since I left Dunfermline. In my first letter, I mentioned having gone about 4,000 miles by sea from Venice to Bombay. Now, I can write about 3,500 miles in my triangular tour of India! For those interested, the rail fare alone cost Rs. 300—that is about £13.15.

Back to the heat of the plains again, where they were waiting for more rains to come. After seeing the rushing torrents and luscious green fields of Kashmir, it was a sorry sight to see the parched land and empty riverbeds.

The annual Bible Women's Retreat was held in Pulivendla, and I was glad to join in this once again. Shortly after my arrival in India last year, I attended a similar gathering so it was good to meet again and practise my Telugu with the women. Many speak no English at all so this was very good for me! As well as listening to some of the Bible Studies and talks, understanding only very little, I was able to join in the singing of lyrics. As the language is phonetic, once the letters are mastered, one can read. I enjoy the singing; though often have no idea what it is all about! Singing is good for me in language study as to some extent the speed is fairly slow and regular, rather than in conversations and church liturgy, which can be gabbled at such a speed that I get lost!

While in Pulivendla, I learned that the Women's Work Committee of the Diocese had recommended that when I finish at the Language School in November I work with Milcamma Isaiah, an Indian lady in charge of training Bible Women and go out with her into the surrounding villages. I am to live in Gooty when I am not out with her.

My holiday finished as it began with a wedding. This time, I was invited to Hyderabad to the wedding of Eileen Bending (C.W.M. missionary) from Adoni, and Kurien Jacob from Kerala, South India. In the ceremony, they had a mixture of Indian and western customs, with the bride wearing a white and silver sari. It was a very happy occasion and gave me the opportunity of meeting with other missionaries for the first time. It was good to see Muriel Harrison who was with me at Carey Hall in my second year.

Then it was back to Bangalore for more language study. This term there were only five of us, of all nationalities—American, Australian, German, English and Scottish—learning two languages—Telugu and Kanarese. Our progress test for this term is already past, and for me, although I passed, it served to show how much I should have known but did not—or could not remember! In our fortnightly orientation lectures, we have heard about the beggar problem in India, the famine in Bihar, demonstrations of Indian dances, to mention only a few subjects covered.

In May this year, a new regulation was issued by the government requiring British Commonwealth missionaries to obtain visas and apply annually for registration to be allowed to stay in the country. Hitherto all missionaries from other countries had this restriction with the exception of Commonwealth countries. Since then, it has been learned that some missionaries have failed in their applications for new or return visas. At the beginning of this month, the newspaper reported that after four or five years, there will be no missionaries working in India. They say the aim is to let Indian church missions take over the educational and hospital work now being done by foreigners.

This year, I will be more used to a hot Christmas instead of a snowy one—and singing Telugu lyrics rather than English carols.

Betty

Letter 4
Visits to Villages in Andhra Pradesh

Gooty, Andhra Pradesh
17 February 1968

Dear Friends,

Greetings for 1968! Sorry, I am so late with them! I had good intentions of writing earlier but this seems to be the jet age as far as time goes. I send my thanks to all those who have written and sent magazines or parcels during the past year. I enjoy reading all the news of Britain through the magazines. I appreciated and enjoyed the parcels of foodstuffs and toiletries etc. Indian children friends are thrilled with their gifts of toys and comics. At Christmas, we visited some villages and gave out old Christmas cards to the children. It was heartrending to see how much this simple gift meant to them. For some, it would be their only present and the glow in their faces as they received something of their very own was quite touching. Some came to the service with the card pinned to their dresses or in their shirt pockets. When I visited a village with another missionary at the beginning of February, the children came running to show us their well-preserved Christmas cards—and that same glow of pride was there. One could see how much they appreciated them.

Owing to a number of factors and the fact that I was not ready for it, I did not sit my second-year written exam in November as I had earlier hoped to do. However, by the time the course ended in mid-November, I had had a good grounding in grammar and in the prescribed books for translation. By this time, I had had enough of language study and was longing to get out into the villages, so at the earliest opportunity, I went off with the Bible Women.

I have been to a number of villages already and enjoy it very much, in spite of being stared at all the time. After a few days in one place, you begin to be accepted and the stares are less frequent. After a seven-mile walk through the fields or a bullock cart ride to another village, it starts all over again! I am in my element with the children—playing games, teaching action choruses (I am very grateful for my Christian Endeavour training here—though now have to teach them in Telugu) or telling my Telugu teacher's version of the Bible stories that I had to learn for my first exam.

The children are great fun and explode into gales of laughter when I make a mistake—much to the consternation of parent onlookers who try to shush them! However, to little avail as I sing a chorus pointing to my ears and saying eyes! I spent Christmas Eve and morning in a village and found it a very humbling experience. (I could almost picture myself back in Bethlehem 2,000 years ago.) In various experiences in India already, I can see myself in Biblical times. After my first two weeks out in villages, I came back to Gooty quite exhausted—both mentally and physically. I am still not immune to the Indian cold germs or tummy accustomed to the hot curries yet, so from time to time I am reminded of this— though not too seriously. Mentally, my head was buzzing with all my new impressions during and after that camp. I kept thinking about what is Christian and what merely western; why some things need to be changed and how other things, strange to us, are nevertheless quite acceptable. There are many things we can learn from Indians. In spite of the language problem, I feel very much at home in the villages and feel welcomed.

As well as village work, I have been attending our Diocesan Council Meetings (in Telugu) and Church of South India Synod in Coimbatore. I thought it a great honour to be appointed as a delegate from the Rayalaseema Diocese to Synod and found the sessions very interesting. It was also a great opportunity to meet all the Bishops and people from other dioceses. Some of the Bishops and Pastors did not impress me very much, though there were a few exceptional ones who will be able to see the Church of South India march forward into the future. As a German visitor said, his church had been going for over 150 years, while the C.S.I. was only 20 years old. This really impressed me and made me stop criticising so much.

We have had a visit from Rev. A.J. Todman, our C.W.M. Mission Secretary for India and as well as personal talks with him we had a three-day retreat with senior church workers in the diocese. During the discussions, I learnt quite a lot about the way some of the pastors think and act. The more I see and hear of some of the malpractices of Christians and church leaders, the more depressed I become. More and more, especially in view of the government's growing desire to see missionaries leave, we are handing over jobs and responsibility to the Indians. It is hard to sit back when we find the work not being done properly, leaders shirking their responsibilities, money or grain meant for projects not being used for the purpose given etc. In the past, the missionaries have been criticised for taking all the responsibility on their shoulders and the Indians merely obeying orders, or giving the Indians the principal posts but still giving the orders from second place. Many Indians should be capable of taking charge themselves—some do and do it well—but many are not ready for responsibility. The extended family system makes it very difficult for a man to refuse to help his relatives with loans (never to be returned) from money or grains entrusted to him for distribution. It is impossible for him to report the malpractices he sees because of his inter-relationship with them. It makes me wonder where their consciences are. It also reminds me of the example I was once given: how people are taught they should not shoot a bird in a sitting position. Who says they have a right to shoot the bird at all? The growing drunkenness in some villages is becoming more and more disturbing, especially as Andhra Pradesh is a Prohibition State. As we were reminded in the Retreat, the church needs to give more guidance and teaching on the Christian life, stewardship etc. The people are seeking something, even if it is just to get out of their present state of poverty and hunger for a few hours. So the Church is challenged to show the way of Christ and to give them a good example to follow and a goal to aim at.

Now, I am out camping in the villages with the divisional chairman, local pastor and Bible Women. They are conducting harvest services when the villagers give their annual contribution to the church. The crops of groundnuts, rice and various grains have been or are being harvested, and the people bring what portion they can afford. After the service, the various items are auctioned and the money set aside for the work of the church. Eggs, hens, grain, fruit and sometimes 'surprise packets' (contents unknown) cause excitement as they are being auctioned.

It is an interesting experience going from village to village, and I am especially enjoying going back to some of the villages I had first visited in November and December. There it is a great thrill to recognise and be recognised, to see how the children have grown. I am also depressed to see how someone is failing or children undernourished; to see four-month old twins, smaller than new born babies, pale, thin and anaemic—being fed on mother's milk only and two—three-year olds still being breast fed. Seeing all this makes me wish I had some nursing training. I hope later, with some vitamin pills, common sense and by trial and error, to do something to help. Please remember all these people in their difficulties and pray that I may be shown what I should do.

Bangalore seems far removed from the Andhra villages, and in spite of the difficulties and frustrations, I much prefer the villages. There are many frustrations but also many joys. I am very grateful to have been led to India to share with the Indians some of their joys and sorrows. In our recent travels on foot and by bullock cart, we have seen the sun rise and set and a full moon rise and set. Nature seems so beautiful and impressive here that I am awed by the wonder of it all and sometimes break into song as we walk through the fields.

On 8 March, I hope to move to Cuddapah to live with Peggy Hawkings and go out to the villages from there. It will be good to open out all my trunks etc. as so far I have been managing with just a few essentials. I shall miss Gooty though, as it has been my home since I came to India—the lovely tank (lake) beside the house, and hilly fort in the centre of the town, which I have climbed several times. No doubt, I will soon find that Cuddapah has its own attractions too.

Some of you have been asking about the recent earthquakes and if I was involved. Fortunately, they seemed to occur in places before and after I visited them but never while I was there! Our area is reputed to be very old geographically, and only minor quakes were felt. Some people were wakened with their beds shaking.

Greetings for Easter and springtime.
Betty

Letter 5
Working with Bible Women
in Cuddapah District

Cuddapah, Andhra Pradesh

27 October 1968

Dear Friends,

It seems such a long time since I wrote my last circular letter, and Christmas is almost here again. This will be my third Christmas in India, and I look forward once again to be celebrating this festival with Indian friends in the sunshine and heat, instead of in the snow. As I write now, the skin is peeling off my arms and neck after being sunburnt last week. No doubt, many of you in the UK at any rate will be well wrapped up in winter woollies. I spent this weekend at Chickballapur with Barbara and Keith Graham. After my annual medical check-up at our mission hospital there, just to prove that I was fit, Barbara and I climbed the Nandi Hill, which is 5,000 feet—and caught the sun. Leslie Robinson is now in Chikka (our abbreviated western version of Chickballapur) too, after coming back from furlough. It was good to have news of Scotland with a Scottish accent!

Let me fill in the gap since February when I last wrote. I was appointed to be in charge of women's work in Cuddapah District, working with two Bible Women. I moved from Gooty to Cuddapah on 8 March to live with Peggy Hawkings. I slowly settled in there, emptying trunks and rearranging rooms etc. Leaving things still not all unpacked, I went off camping to one of the villages in Pulivendla district where I had been working since leaving Bangalore. This time, we were holding an adult literacy course for the men of the village. They were so eager to learn and would be waiting on the church doorstep before we got up in the morning, ready for a lesson before going to work. Then back they came again in the evening for more. I was a bit flummoxed when my first pupil was a deaf and dumb man, so I was really tested! We resorted to hand signals and stick drawings to get the meaning across, and he came eagerly to all sessions. Just as I was made to realise that this man had a brain and understanding and was intelligent, and though physically dumb was by no means mentally so, so too as we worked with these illiterate villagers I soon learned that their ignorance was only in reading letters and not in knowledge or mental ability. Yet so often in our very use of the word 'illiterate' we conjure up a picture of hopelessness. They just had never been taught nor had the opportunity to learn. With their natural gift for singing, we would sing lyrics, listing all the advantages of being able to read and write, and once more it was I who learned such a lot, and came to realise how much I took reading and writing for granted. Have you ever stopped to think what it would be like if you had to ask your Town Councillor to write your letters for you—especially if you couldn't trust him not to add comments of his own? Or not to be able to read the prices in shop windows, or see if your bill or receipt was for the correct amount; not to be able to read the newspaper and with no radio or T.V. as a substitute but having to depend on having the news passed round by word of mouth—and you know how distorted that can be sometimes! For these Indians their greatest ambition was to be able to read the Bible for themselves, though these other advantages would prove useful too. I am often struck by their great longing to own and be able to read the Bible. Some new literates eagerly read Gospel portions, pamphlets, or texts but are never fully satisfied until they can read the BIBLE and possess one of their own. I was very humbled recently when I visited a village, half of which had been destroyed by a fire only two weeks previously. Many lost their homes, the grain they had stored for the year, chickens and animals, their few clothes and other possessions. However, it was for Bibles they came and asked—as this previous possession had been lost.

As I left the village after two weeks of adult literacy work, bumping along the rough track in a bullock cart in the hot sunshine, I suddenly felt very tired and weak—and a few days later was in bed with jaundice (though it was some time before I changed colour and jaundice was diagnosed!) There I remained for about two weeks, not enjoying this enforced rest in the least. I was able to be up on Easter Sunday and on that day was officially welcomed into the membership and fellowship of Cuddapah town church. Then it was soon time to head to the hills for our summer holidays, and I really felt in need of it. I travelled with Gwen Morris to Kodaikanal and enjoyed the bus journey up the twisting hairpin bends into the mountains. Many Missionary Societies have houses there in a beautiful setting of lake and mountains. Living at 7,500 feet, we really felt on top of the world. Although there was no snow, it was very cold at this altitude. and it took some time to be acclimatised after the heat of the plains.

It was good to meet more of our missionaries from other parts of India, and friends from other Societies. As well as enjoying the beauty of the countryside, we were entertained by plays, musical evenings and a superb performance of the Sound of Music put on by the students of the local school. The different mission industries had several displays and sales of their various wares, including lace, embroidered linens, toys, baskets etc. I had daily Telugu lessons and attempted the exam in May, but it only proved to show that I was not yet ready for it. All too soon, it was time to return to Cuddapah and into a succession of retreats and summer schools.

The first of them was in Cuddapah for the women from the surrounding villages in the district. Over 100 came, and I enjoyed helping in a small way with this. It was a real holiday for these women who for a change had food prepared for them and no family responsibilities. Many could be found in little clusters, talking or singing well into the night. Then on to a smaller similar gathering for the women in Pulivendla where I had been working since leaving Language School. I was sorry to be leaving that district so soon after getting to know the villagers and children—and how to get to some of the out-of-the-way places!

The Bible Women and women workers in our diocese have an annual retreat when we meet for Bible study and refreshment, exchange methods and learn new ideas etc. This year, we went to Machilipatnam in the north of Andhra Pradesh. On our first day, we went to the sea, which many were seeing for the first time. It sounded very grand to say afterwards that we had been swimming in the Bay of Bengal! The Indian women contented themselves with hitching up their saris and paddling, but Peggy and I donned pyjamas (for modesty or propriety's sake) and got right into the sea. This year we joined with those from Krishna Godavari (one of the other dioceses in this State) so we had the advantage of having fellowship with others engaged in the same work and comparing notes on our method of working.

Perhaps, I should say something about women's work in our diocese. The diocese is divided into ten divisions with a Minister in charge of each division. He oversees all the ministerial, pastoral and evangelistic work in his area. The Bishop of course is over all. We have about 23 Indian Bible Women working, usually in pairs, in the diocese. The custom in India is to keep the sexes separate in many things. The ministers usually work with the men, apart from conducting services when families come. The women sit apart, at the back or to one side. Bible Women and women missionaries work with the women and children. At present, I am working with two Bible Women in 19 villages in the Cuddapah district. There is opportunity to work in many other areas when the time permits. These villages range from a mere handful of houses to 70 families or more. In our diocese the Christians are mainly 'outcast' Indians and very poor. They live in their community separate from the main village where the higher caste Hindus live. Sometimes, the Christian houses are completely separate, with a field or road in between them and the Hindus, but often they are simply in a corner of the main village. Many of our people work as coolies in the fields belonging to the Hindus. This includes men, women and children, all working to try to support the family. They earn a mere one or two rupees per day WHEN there is work. We are in a famine area and often the rains fail, and there is no work for the people. They have to borrow at heavy rates of interest from the moneylenders. More of this another time.

Those of us who are village workers are expected to go camping at least 15 days in the month and the rest of the time is taken up with committees, correspondence, preparations, plus all the other jobs landed on the missionary. The Bible Women camp for 15–20 days per month. Of the pair, one of them has usually had some Bible training and is in charge, while the other is a helper and sees to the cooking but generally helps in many ways. When I mention camping no doubt tents will spring to mind. That was the abode of the earlier missionaries involved in village work. Now, we usually 'camp out' in the village school-cum-church. This can vary from a beautiful stone building with tiled roof and paved floor, to a mud hut with a thatched roof going bare in places, earth floor and straw matting door held together with rope. We bring our own food supplies, lamps and bedding. We are fortunate in Cuddapah to have a jeep to get around in—otherwise, we have to depend on buses. These are overcrowded at the best of times and liable to rattle past without stopping when they see us and our pile of luggage! Sometimes we go by bullock cart, or walk to get from place to place. The usual routine—though as I said before, nothing is usual or routine—once we arrive in the village, is to visit all the homes, enquiring about the family and so on. Peggy has found it useful to make a map of the village, draw up a census, and so keep a record of the families. This is added to or subtracted from as someone is born or dies or is married and given away to another village. We bring medicines with us for sale and set up a clinic. People come with simple sores (some not so simple but horrible ulcerated masses of pus) and complaints, and we do our best to help, or write them a note to take to the nearest hospital. I often wish I knew more in the medical line in order to diagnose and help more. I hope to learn by experience, as others have had to do. We also take tracts, gospels, Bibles and books for sale and hang them in a display holder on a central tree or convenient wall. The children soon come swarming and hand over their 1 or 2 naya paisa for a pamphlet or 10 naya paisa (about one and a half pence) for a gospel. Sometimes, we even resort to the old barter system and give books in exchange for a handful of peanuts or measure of grain. In the afternoon after school, we play games with the children, teach choruses, tell Bible stories and act out parables etc. In the evenings when the adults and older children return from work in the fields, and after they have eaten, we hold a service. Sometimes, this is preceded by a bajanna. This is a procession round the houses singing Christian lyrics as they go and calling the people to worship. To this service come many Hindus and especially if it is held outside, they come in their crowds— usually not wanting to commit themselves but eager to listen. They stay in the shadows or crowd in the doorway of the church. The Hindus come for books and gospels and medicines etc. too. When we stay for more than one day in a village, more specific teaching and instruction can be given to the women and children and some adult literacy work done too. It is hoped that two or three visits at least can be made per year to each village to encourage the congregations while the pastor of the district is expected to make monthly visits for communion, baptism, teaching etc.

During September, each year there is a special programme and offerings take for the work of overseas mission. Several years ago, a pastor from this diocese went to Papua as the first missionary of the Church of South India. He has since died, but now there is another Indian family working in Thailand. Indians too are going forth with the gospel, as well as receiving for themselves, and this is how it should be. I am sure our churches at home would be revived if some of the Indian Christians came into their midst.

A three-week adult literacy course is held annually in Gooty in July for the women of the diocese. Having been inspired by the other course in Yene and seeing the worthwhile achievements after such a short time, I was eager to do more. Over 100 women came to Gooty, some new literates as teachers. It is true that the best way to learn is to teach. As a teacher, I certainly learnt a lot. As well as reading classes, there were Bible studies, singing, games and drama sessions. Peggy had just returned from a course on drama and enthusiastically inspired us to improvise a drama on the life of Dorcas. As a result, the Bible became alive to some in a way they had never experienced before. It was good to be back in my old home in Gooty again, climb the fort and walk along the tank bund.

After we returned to Cuddapah, after all these various courses and camps, Peggy and I got busy on the garden to see what could be done. Until recently, we had constantly to be on our guard to see that our garden gate was always latched properly otherwise, the goats were in enjoying our best shrubs. We had a special goat-proof swing-type gate put in. At first, it kept out people. The opening was made too narrow and only the thinnest could come through easily! This was soon put to rights and now even our portly visitors can call once again! Now, a family of monkeys on the compound seem to be getting all they want from the Bishop's garden so are not robbing us of our plants. Enthusiastically we planted seeds in pots and daily watched their growth. After remodelling the garden, with a circular central bed and four corner plots, we anxiously waited for the rain to come and the right moment to transplant. We planted tomatoes and roselles as well as a variety of flowers. We hope they escape the attention of the monkeys and squirrels so we can enjoy them. I hear from Peggy that the flowers are now blooming and some have been picked for indoor use.

Unfortunately, I had to leave to come to Bangalore for language study so 1 am missing seeing the progress. I have two months' study leave to prepare for the second year Telugu exam beginning on 5 November. I have mixed feelings about being back in this big city of one and a half million people, including many Europeans. I felt quite lost and lonely when I first returned here after the friendly contacts in the villages and simpler way of life there, and long to be back in their midst again. What must the village Indian think too when he comes to a city like this for the first time, or to seek work?

Depression is said to be one of the symptoms of jaundice and I have had my share of this in plenty recently. I have experienced frustration and worry, helplessness and loneliness too, and it was only when I reached rock bottom a few days ago that I found I had been trying to do things in my own strength alone. Now, I know how impossible it is to live without faith. Psalm 42 and Psalm 139 really mean something to me now as I have lived them. I found a book by Reuel L. Howe—*Man's Need and God's Action* spoke to my needs just then and was very helpful. Talking of books, perhaps some of you may be interested in the following books on India that I have recently read. These give some good pictures of Indian scenes and ways of life:

An Area of Darkness by V.S. Naipaul – 1964
Hunting the Guru by Anne Marshall – 1963
The Wind Cannot Read by Richard Mason – 1947 (novel)
Verdict on India by Beverley Nichols – 1944
The Maneater of Mongudi by R.K. Narayan – 1963

Now before this letter gets any longer, I *had* better stop. Many thanks to all who have written to me, sent magazines, books, comics and old Christmas cards. I am always glad to hear from you all with news of your doings in other parts of the world. I enjoy reading the magazines and papers. These are passed on to other colleagues and Indian friends and much appreciated by them too.

This comes with early Christmas greetings and good wishes to you all, wherever you may be.

Betty

Letter 6
My Feelings

Dear Friends,

I have just come back to Cuddapah after five days' camping in one of the villages in this district. I first visited this particular village in December 1968 and understood that no missionary had ever been there before, so it was all very new. I went there a little bit afraid of the unknown. Would there be lots of drunken fights, party quarrelling etc.? This time friends greeted me. The women and children came rushing to welcome us when the jeep approached. All the faces were so familiar this time. I must confess I could not remember many of their names! About the second day there, I began to think of all the adjectives to describe how I felt...happy, embarrassed, annoyed, helpless, frustrated, angry and impatient, only to mention a few.

Happy – at being back and receiving such a genuine welcome.

Embarrassed – at being feted. This came about because on my last visit, I sent a very sick man to the hospital with cholera, and this timely action saved his life. He was full of praise and I hardly recognised the fit young man who came to me all smiles, compared to the cold, dying skeleton of a creature I had helped into the jeep. I was presented with a large garland of flowers, then taken on a tour of the village at 10 pm. I was led by a band, consisting of three flat drums beaten with thin sticks, and a small kettledrum, beaten with leather pads. Every few yards, the procession stopped, a bundle of straw set alight and the drums heated over it. This I gather was to improve the tone though it made no appreciable difference to me.

At the various stops, I was asked to sit in a large wooden armchair while the young men put on a display of skill. To me, it looked like the twirling done by the leader of a Scottish pipe band, only the stick was much longer. Then the men did a mixture of a Morris Dance and fencing with their sticks. This is called a 'Tiger Dance'. Then followed weight lifting. A huge boulder was lifted from the ground, onto the stomach, up to the right shoulder, and then dropped over the back. This reminded me of tossing the caber in Scotland. On another few yards and the same performance was repeated. Sometimes, quite young boys tried their hand. When we reached Rajanna's house I was given their thank-offering to God (two rupees, beetle nuts and leaves) and was called upon to pray and give the benediction. These proceedings had come as a complete surprise and I was unprepared for any of it, including this solemn ceremony. When taking a service I like to have everything written down in front of me to make sure I get the Telugu fairly right but no time for this now. I somehow got the expected message across. I am sure I made many grammatical mistakes as I made up the sentences as I went along. By 11:15 pm, I was ready to excuse myself and get to bed, having been on the go since 6 am, but they insisted on escorting me home, with the same stops as before.

Annoyed – at the way a village school is run, and the bad example and witness to Christians and others, of a Christian headmaster and his wife. I understand that what I saw is common to many of our village schools. I am amazed that the children learn as much as they do, with no proper lessons and everything simply learned off by heart. Numbers and tables were chanted at great speed, but there was difficulty in doing simple sums. I asked four ten-year-old boys to write an account of the happenings of the previous night (the procession etc.) as this was my first experience of such a display. I gather that this ritual is performed at festival times and weddings too. When the first one brought me a messy bit of paper with rubbed out letters, I asked him to read it out to me. I found he did not know half of the words, even though he assured me he had written it himself. When the second boy produced exactly the same account, I asked if he had copied the story from a book. He said, "No," but that his teacher had written it for him. I questioned the teacher about giving the boys the piece to copy, but he said it was only meant as a guide. The boys had been told to write it in their own words. The children are so used to not thinking for themselves that they could only reproduce what was before them. And so on…up through the schools and universities, set answers are learned and poured forth for examinations.

Helpless – at the sight of so many sick people, especially those suffering from T.B. and knowing that they are too poor to afford treatment. At first, I was annoyed that they had not gone to the hospital sooner but realised that many had no money for the bus fare. They would either have to borrow at heavy rates of interest or wait months until they could earn enough to save even a little. In many cases, too, although the Government Hospitals are supposed to give free treatment, many ward boys and nurses will do nothing until they are given a tip. One of our village women leaders died recently of cancer of the mouth. When she eventually went to Vellore Hospital, the doctors told her that, had she come a few months sooner, she might have been cured. Her only comment was, "It's always too late for the poor." There are so many poor in India just like her. Daily I had queues of men, women and children, Christians, Hindus and Muslims, coming for medicines and treatment. We sell iron and vitamin pills etc. at cost price, and most people can afford to pay for them. Our bringing them to the village saves them their bus fare to hospital. They have great faith in anything the Missamma (lady missionary) prescribes. I hope this makes up for any wrong diagnosis I make. I don't think an overdose of vitamins would kill anyone! Would it? Medical friends, please advise! Wounds and scabies etc. we dress and treat freely while we are in the villages. The improvement after a few dressings is quite amazing. One man came to me this time with his hand swollen to twice its normal size. It was covered in dried manure and leaves and I could not see the wound properly. He said it had been swollen like this for several weeks. Five days ago the pus had begun to come pouring out. I covered the lot with our famous 'cure-all' black ichthyol ointment (ichthammol). The next day I was about knocked flat by the smell when I took off the dressing. I don't know if it was the manure ripening under the ointment, or gangrene or what—the former I hope. The sight of a huge hole out of which a mass of pus had come just about finished me. I pressed on for what else to do? Another dose of ichthyol to clean out more mess and I advised him to go to the hospital. No! Back he came several more times with no signs of going to the hospital. Festering eyes and ears there are in plenty, from young babies to the elderly. These too get daily squeezes of ointment that miraculously heal them up in a short time. How I wish I knew more and could do more in this village clinic type of work. Our mission hospitals are so understaffed and overworked that they cannot get out to the villages, as they would like.

And so it goes on…anger and impatience, joy and a sense of feeling one is in the right job, a constant sense of un-fittedness and yet knowing there is no-one else to do the job. I can always remember Rev. D. P. Thomson saying, "Don't wait until you are perfect. Get on and the way will be shown." Therefore, I go on, being wonderfully guided in both small and large steps. I often think of saying, "Necessity is the mother of invention." I have proved this to be true many times; using a clean piece of toilet paper as the backing in a dressing when the lint runs out; sticking awkward places with Sellotape when the bandages won't stretch that far; using a piece of broken-down whitewashed wall as chalk, to write on the blackboard when the teacher couldn't produce any; turning a bed into a screen behind which one could have a little privacy when bathing, or using it as a book display or medicine counter…and so on.

After the evening services each night we divided into groups, with Elia our driver in charge of the men and myself and the Bible Women in charge of the women. We tried to produce a play for the last evening, bringing the parable up to date, with everyone improvising with his or her own words after working out the rough plan. We have tried this several times now and the result is amazingly good after only a few rehearsals. Every time we find some member of the cast can't come, so we have to find a substitute, even on the last night! I am sure the Bible comes alive to the people as they enact the scenes, even if the finished product is not as polished as a theatre show. The women did the 'Good Samaritan', with one woman going off to our Adult Literacy Course and being attacked on the way, robbed of her gold earrings, bangles, rings and necklace etc. Along came another two Christian women on their way to the Course, but they are afraid of what may happen to them if they stop. They hurry on their way. Then a cook and her assistant pass by. The latter wants to stop and lend a hand but the cook says they must hurry and get the food ready for all the people coming to the Course. Then two Muslim women come near, and like the Good Samaritan, they stop, take care of the injured woman's wounds, take her to the coffee shop and leave her there for a few days until they return, pay the bill and escort her home. Last night the men did the story of the 'Lost Son' and were very realistic. The young village boy is tired of helping in his father's fields. He is keen to see the cinema and the bright lights of the city etc. and we know the rest. Giving Indian names and settings does make it come alive, and isn't it true that participation is the best means of learning?

Now back to office work and accounts, and the 101 other jobs in the bungalow. This evening's leisure activity for Peggy and me was moving a mound of manure from outside the garden gate to inside. Normally there are many hostel boys playing around and we hoped to make use of their eagerness to help in any ploy. Tonight not a soul was in sight. Peggy and I carried basins full of the stuff into the garden while Jeevaiah filled the basins. Towards the end, we had three little helpers who puffed and heaved with each load, and soon all the manure was inside the garden. Our next ploy is to re-pot some of our plants and get the garden ready for planting seeds when the rains come. We have had a few showers of late but hope for a lot more.

I suppose you have all read in the newspapers about the Telangana troubles in and around Hyderabad. The Telangana people, formerly belonged to a little State of their own. Now, it is part of Andhra Pradesh. They want to be independent and are going to any lengths to try to force the Government to give them their desire. Some people tell me it is just like Scotland wanting its independence from England.

Peggy is calling me now to help her with the Manchester Guardian crossword puzzle. This is one of our hobbies—though it looks more like a full-time occupation when you see us at the table with a dictionary, encyclopaedia, Roget's Thesaurus, and historical books of dates and events etc. That and a little bit of intuition or guesswork, and we just about manage to complete the puzzle before next week's paper comes!

Bed is calling, as well as a crossword clue to think about, as I stop for now. I realise this is only a little snippet of my news but thought you might like to have fuller details about village experiences, rather than a list of comings and goings.

Betty

Letter 7
Adventures by Jeep or Bullock Cart

Cuddapah, Andhra Pradesh
29 March 1970

Dear Friends,

It is too late to wish you a Happy Christmas now, or even a Happy New Year, as a quarter of it has gone already! However, I do send Easter Greetings. Easter is also a time of new beginnings—and for me, new resolutions. I had hoped to write after Christmas and give you the news of our activities then, but what with one thing and another, I did not make it.

Just before Christmas, I was elected as Treasurer of the Diocese. I really felt that this was not what I should be doing at this time. I would be tied to an office desk and not be able to do any village work etc. which I was originally called to do. In these past few years, I have been turning my hand to a variety of tasks and learning many new things, all of which I felt were parts going to make up a whole pattern. However, to take on the treasurership was a completely new pattern altogether. The work really calls for a qualified accountant. It was not easy to say 'no'. It took a lot of heart-searching, and my mind was full of questions. Did I have the right to refuse? Was I shirking responsibility? There were people pulling me in both directions, but just as many believed I would be given the strength to do the job, I believe I was given the strength to say 'No'. As the days go on I am more sure than ever that this was the right decision—especially now when I am out camping in the villages.

When I last wrote, I told you of village experiences. During this camp, I felt that there are more things I could share with you. A few weeks ago, Peggy and I set off on a 'double' camp. She and her two Bible Women were going to villages on one side of the main road and my two Bible Women and I were to be working down the opposite side, with the jeep ferrying back and forth between us each

44

day, moving our equipment. Last year we did this when out collecting grain for our village women's Summer Schools, so it was no new experience, in general, that is—as there were plenty of new 'additional extras' as we soon found out! Santhoshamma and Shanthamma my Bible Women were instructed to get on a bus to the first village. We were shocked to find them still standing at the roadside as we passed through a town on the way! There was a big festival in a distant city and all the buses were packed full and did not stop. The jeep was already full to overflowing with luggage and six people. In spite of the fact that the jeep has had a major repair and we had been warned not to overload, everyone was eager to squash up to leave room (?) for the two! However, I had to be firm and say 'No'. What to do? Finally, we succeeded in getting Elia the driver and Jeevaiah our servant onto a lorry going in the same direction, and I drove the jeep and its load. Elia stood up in the lorry and kept an eye on me, signalling directions as we went along in case I didn't know what to do! As we went along we passed a circus procession with camels pulling a trailer, and I commented on this. Mariamma, one of my Bible Woman interrupted me with, "Mother, don't talk, keep your eyes on the road!" So much for my driving! The way it came across in Telugu was much more expressive!

As usual, we were welcomed in all the villages we visited and urged to stay longer than one day. We had several scorpion stings to treat. It is amazing there are not more as most of the villagers go barefoot. Usually, the patients arrive after we are all settled in bed for the night, or as in one case, just as we were ready to begin the service. A father came into the church and said his daughter had been stung on the leg. Would I come to the house? Off he went and I began to mix 15 drops of medicine in a glass of water. Just then in came a girl crying hysterically and her mother saying a scorpion had stung her. I thought this was my patient and dosed her only to turn around to find the father who had come earlier, urging me to hurry up! This medicine requires three doses at ten-minute intervals. I was kept busy going back and forth between the two patients and trying to keep them calm and at the same time exercise the stung limbs. As I mixed the second dose, someone let out a shriek and there at my feet was a huge scorpion. Fortunately, it was quickly disposed of before I became a patient too! Never a dull moment!

Sometimes on this tour, it was easier to go by bullock cart where the villages were close to one another. When I first started camping, this was our only means of transport. I was well used to rumbling along dusty rocky roads, perched up high on top of all our luggage. At one place instead of crossing a little bridge, the bullocks headed straight for the river and bent down to drink! That action had us off our perches and spread-eagled all over the cart. Shanthamma opted to get down altogether while the bullocks were yoked properly again and we made our way through the river and up the other bank. She decided it was safer to walk the rest of the way too but I was quite happy to sit tight. We arrived safely.

We finished our ten-day camp and all met together for a picnic lunch in a little wood. In this cool and peaceful spot, Peggy and I worked out all our camp accounts for books, medicines and harvest collections. Then we took part in the laying of the foundation stone of a new church nearby. As the sun was setting and the sky was tinged with red, we gave thanks to God as the Bishop laid the first stone and threw earth on top.

I am in camp again for Easter after a spell back in Cuddapah when I was dealing with hostel matters. We have recently had a new water pipe installed for the hostel bathroom through a gift of money from Germany. Water had been trickling through very slowly. It takes an age to get action from the Water Department, but finally something is happening—if only to say that a whole new stretch of pipeline has to be laid. This may help the flow of water, we are told!

More free foodstuffs arrived at the hostel and as the boys all helped to carry the sacks from the lorry to the storeroom there was a real spirit of unity and co-operation as they worked in teams to lift the heavy loads. There were great puffs and groans as they heaved and collapsed in a heap. A real sense of achievement as the last bag was put in place.

It was a quick move from this happy atmosphere to my first village in this camp where there was an air of sadness and worry. Almost every house had at least one smallpox patient and two children had died. The people believe that no medicine should be given until the fever passes. During this time, the patient is not given a bath, as the water would spread the disease. At least two children's eyes were affected, and they had lost their sight. They were a pathetic sight. Another patient was brought to me, and it was hard to believe that the skeleton was two years old. It was heart-breaking to hear that this family had lost three children some time ago from fever and another one from smallpox only a few days ago. A six-year-old daughter was still suffering from smallpox and this two-year-old from malnutrition. What to do? The government keeps urging people to limit their families to two or three at the most and family planning notices are seen everywhere and even on stamps. Sterilisation operations on men and women are performed in most hospitals and the government pays the patients who come for this. In some places, they are now advertising that they will give a transistor radio to those who come forward. This modern status symbol may be a draw to many.

This was my first time out in the villages for Easter, and like Christmas, we spent in a village; this too was very meaningful—simple, yet so much more like the real thing. So often Christian festivals in big cities are swamped by the 'extras'—decorations and feasts, and the real festival is crowded out. On Saturday night, when we went to sleep out in the open, the blackness above us was lit by bright twinkling stars. To me, they symbolised hope and a promise of good tidings to come. We need not worry about the darkness. This was heralding the new day ahead. Easter morning we all woke early with the moon still shining brightly above us and in a short time we saw the sky lighten, then turn to red as the golden ball of sun appeared on the horizon. What more decoration did we need than these, the wonderful works of our Creator?

This was a small congregation but the very smallness was impressive. The night before, I had noticed a polished stone slab lying on top of the rough-hewn stone communion table. In the early morning, as two men came and carried it away, it was just like the stone being rolled away from the sepulchre (I discovered later that, unasked, they had put it there and were now asking Rs. 25 for it and the congregation were refusing to pay!) After our short service, we distributed handfuls of puffed rice, lentil type seeds, brown sugar and a grain mixture, which the people had brought as an offering. This was washed down with sugar-cane juice. There was a real sense of fellowship and at-oneness as we shared in this simple meal together. Then off to Rameswaram where we joined in a town church Easter communion service and afterwards had lunch with the Pastor and his family.

In this happy atmosphere, it is hard to believe that the diocese is involved in so many court cases, and so much time and money are being spent in this way. Some of our church members feel they have been wronged and in their desire for power, intend to fight at all costs. Perhaps it is a sign of the times as there is unrest in the country at large—indeed in the whole world and strikes are common. Now, the banks, hospitals and government offices are all on strike and causing great hardship to many. As we lived through the darkness of Good Friday and Saturday and came through to rejoice in Easter Day with its promise of hope for the future, we press on, knowing that better days lie ahead.

Betty

Letter 8
Children's New Life Centres
and Travels to North India

Cuddapah, Andhra Pradesh
3 February 1971

Dear Friends,

Am I still in time to wish you a Happy New Year? Maybe I had better start by wishing you a Happy Easter, as with the present postal strike this may not reach you for some time! It will soon be a year since I wrote a circular letter. I hope that some news has been trickling through to you in other ways. I have more than enough to do in one day and personal things get pushed aside until I am forced to make time. Now, for some of the highlights of last year.

Children's New Life Centres

One of the most interesting new experiments we have started is our Children's New Life Centre in a village near Cuddapah. This is a hostel with a difference. We have 25 children (both boys and girls) aged between six and nine years, and they have come in groups of five or so from their villages to stay in this hostel for a period of two years. In that time they will be taught to read and write and given a general education with handcrafts, gardening, health etc. as well as Bible teaching. This is intended to make them better leaders in their villages when they grow up. So many children are struggling through school, failing or just scraping their way through innumerable exams and then at the end find it almost impossible to get a job. Unemployment is so great throughout India at present—even for graduates. We feel that illiteracy must be wiped out but that a middle path must be found so that there are educated villagers working in the fields who remain in their villages and try to raise the standards there, instead of moving out to the cities and adding to the unemployed masses there. So many of our boys in the hostel, after six or seven years in school, say they can't do coolie work after they leave, as they have to learn this while young. Many also have the notion of a white-collar job, and ploughing fields and harvesting crops is not appealing to them.

Therefore, this Centre was started with this background and we are amazed and thrilled at its success so far. Within a month these children who have never been to school until now, are able to read and write and are so eager to study. Now, after six months our 'citizens of the future' are shaping up nicely. What a difference in the teaching methods. We have two retired teachers looking after them and teaching them. With 25 pupils instead of the usual 90–100 in our schools (from first class upwards), they can give individual attention and use a variety of interesting methods. The children are taught to think for themselves both in their reading, writing and in their sums. So often, we hear the classes in our compound here chanting off their tables, reciting lines of reading material etc. like parrots—all geared to the exam system and form of questioning. Ask them a question in any other form and you are met with a blank look! Our youngsters are learning their sums through counting shopping bills, change from bus tickets etc. and even working out trick sums that are intended to make them think. Example: If there are 20 birds in a tree and a farmer shot one, how many are left? When this question was asked recently while I was there, eager hands shot up with the answer, '19' but one indignant thinker pronounced 'None' in an emphatic way and proceeded to say why! (Answer at the end of my letter if you haven't worked it out!) Their teaching is related to their village life and in simple ways, we hope to introduce through them, better methods that can help to improve their conditions at home. Many people all over India are looking to our Centre as this is the first experiment of its kind. The Centre is being supported by Kindernothilfe in Germany and other Centres may be opened in other areas after the first set of children leave to return to their villages and work in the fields etc.

Lucknow

In September, I went to Lucknow to Literacy House. There, representatives from all over India gathered under the auspices of the National Christian Council to discuss Functional Literacy and to see the courses provided in this Centre. I gave a report on our Children's New Life Centre, as we believe that this is functional literacy. The main feature of the Literacy House compound is the building in the centre called the House of Prayer for all People. There is glass all around, and a pointed thatched roof and inside on three levels of wooden circular steps, the worshippers face the centre in which there is a cool fountain of water. Muslim, Hindu and Christian forms of prayer are conducted and also periods of silent meditation. As the staff of Literacy House are from different faiths and backgrounds, this time together every morning brings out the unity in diversity.

At the end of the week's seminar, we met Mrs Welthy H. Fisher, the founder of Literacy House—now in her 91st year. She is an amazing person, devoted to the eradication of illiteracy and travels all over the world encouraging people to 'each one teach one'. We did not see Lucknow at its best as we were there during the heavy rains and shared in the suffering of flooding in the grounds, wading knee-deep through the paths to the lecture rooms, with the electricity off for several days, no water to drink or for bathing facilities. Our ingenuity was brought out as we collected water in buckets as it dripped or poured from the roof, or collected it from the channels at the side of the flowerbeds.

Nagpur

On the return journey, I stopped at Nagpur to visit the Headquarters of the National Christian Council and to see the Cathedral. It was on 29 November, Advent Sunday that the Church of North India (C.N.I.) was inaugurated in Nagpur Cathedral. The Church of South India has come through many difficulties in her lifetime but continues to inspire other united churches to be formed. As the C.S.I. plans to unite with Lutherans in the near future to become the Church of Christ in India, we look forward to the day when the North and South may be united and that there will be one united Church in India in the not too far distant future.

Furlough

Peggy left on 1 September 1970 on furlough and a lot of her work has been passed on to me, which gives me less time than ever. Many of you will have met her and heard of our work here. I am looking forward to her return to India in June and a few months together before I go on furlough at the beginning of October.

Camping

With so many extra office responsibilities, I have not been able to do much camping in the villages until just before Christmas. Then it was a joy to get out and be with the villagers as they were preparing for Christmas. Everyone does a 'spring-clean' then. Cracks in the walls are patched, re-roofing is done if necessary, and the house inside and out whitewashed. There is a great hive of activity, especially as the festival day draws near and the extra decorations are added. In one village, I sat enthralled watching rehearsals of a dance. I had just been reading a book about Morris dancing and felt that this had some link with it. There is a circle overhead, suspended from two poles, from which come 20 coloured strands.

Then in the dance (rather like the Maypole without the central pole) the dancers standing in a circle with the cords in their hands, weave in and out to form a pigtail. There were several versions of twists in the different dances. As I sat and watched the dainty footsteps of these big, burly farmers and coolies, I could see their concentration, enjoyment, pride and total absorption in the dance. There was a real sense of teamwork as they each had their place and part to play in making the pattern complete. I sat till almost midnight watching them, then wrapped up in my sleeping bag as the nights are quite chilly in December—well, chilly at 60°, for us used to temperatures in the 90s and 100s. I thought of these village leaders or elders, many of them illiterate, and then of the leaders in our town churches who often only co-operate to make trouble, in their desire for power. We can learn so much from the villagers and their natural built-in abilities.

This made me go on to think about India today and all the changes in all fields. In spite of so much poverty and hardship, there is increasing wealth. This can be seen in the many buildings going up—big stone houses, factories, cinemas etc. Where previously there was only a track, now there are proper roads with buses and lorries plying alongside the bullock carts, rickshaws and donkeys. In the cities, there is air-conditioning and running water, yet in the villages, many live in mud huts or canvas shelters with water several furlongs away in a muddy canal or deep well from which it has to be laboriously hauled.

Status Symbols

Recently interviewing candidates for hostel warden's posts, I was struck by the young people's ideas of what 'education' and 'status' means to them. Coming from their villages where next to no clothes are worn—usually, a shirt and cloth wrapped around the waist—these graduates and college boys now sport tight trousers, pointed shoes, sun-glasses and many also wear spectacles, have a watch and carry a briefcase. Many also have a transistor radio, which blares forth as they walk along the road. For the ladies —many 'with it' young misses are having their long hair cut short and styled at the hairdressers, or their long hair twisted into exotic creations of ringlets and curls. Nylon saris are seen everywhere as they need no ironing; red-painted finger and toenails, and a handbag to carry—and the inevitable sunspecs.

Travelling

Travelling is very cheap in India—about tuppence a mile by train (third class) and about a penny a mile by bus—though the latter usually works out better at one shilling per hour of travel! There always seems to be masses of people on the move—going long distances as well as short. Bombay to Madras is quite common on our railway line through Cuddapah. The luggage taken by the travellers is a remarkable sight in spite of the notices advising people to travel light. Bedding rolls with mattress, sheets, pillow, tiffin carriers (Indian equivalent to picnic hampers), clothes, household goods including very often, large brass water pots etc. A traveller need never starve on his journey as there is always food on sale at the stations or on the train as vendors come aboard and go from carriage to carriage. Some of the agile nip through the windows or doors and clamber through into the next compartment while the train is speeding along, balancing their baskets of oranges, bananas or peanuts as they go. Most stations sell cups of tea or coffee and light refreshments or meals wrapped up in leaves. On many trains, railway-catering staff take orders for meals and these are put on the train and delivered to the compartments on stainless steel trays. A curry meal with the various side dishes and bottle of water can cost less than two shillings and a full western meal (chicken or mutton) in the restaurant car (on some trains only) costs less than five shillings.

Handkerchief

I have been noticing the versatile uses of the common handkerchief. It seems to be used for a variety of purposes, more than for its original intended use. It is used to flick off the dust on a train or bus seat before the wearer of tight white trousers or dhoti eases himself onto the seat. Sometimes, if the place is still considered not quite clean enough it is spread out as a mat on the seat to be sat upon. It can be used to reserve a seat on a bus or train while the occupant is absent. It amazes me that this is usually respected by seat seekers and never removed or stolen. It is used to protect the head from the sun's rays, worn triangular fashion with the ends tucked in the ears if not long enough to tie under the chin! It is used to hold a variety of eatables bought when the purchaser has no other container. The goods, be they limes, oranges, grapes, peanuts, sweets or eggs are placed in the centre of the handkerchief and the first two corners knotted together, followed by the next two. Very occasionally, it is used for the purpose for which it was designed. A good strong blow and two fingers squeezed and flicked at the right angle, is quite sufficient for many!

Church

At Christmas, along with members from other churches in Cuddapah, I joined the local Anglican Church choir, which was leading a service of English carols on Christmas Sunday. The Anglican Bishop, now a Bishop in the Church of North India, gave the sermon and the service was recorded and excerpts broadcast on 25 December.

It was good to sing the well-known and not so well known English carols, though many Telugu lyrics are very beautiful. Christmas Eve, I spent in an orphanage with the children and took part in their Christmas tree celebrations. I arrived at Gooty at midnight in time to wish Pat Roberts a Happy Christmas. After a few days there, we went to Hyderabad and ushered in the New Year in this Muslim city, which is becoming very modernised.

From there to Medak to see the huge cathedral, that looks so incongruous right out in the wilderness. It looks as if it had come from some English parish. It has three beautiful stained glass windows depicting the birth, resurrection and ascension of our Lord, and there is a real atmosphere of worship and reverence in this large house of prayer. Many Hindu patients in the mission hospital on the compound come and give thanks for healing there.

I had heard that Medak was noted for its cathedral and cows! So the next stop was across to the cowshed where about 20 Jersey cows and many calves were to be seen. They looked so healthy and full of milk compared to the local half-starved skin and bone cows and buffaloes. In many parts of India, various countries are sending their best animals to try and improve the strain of animals here. These cows came from Ireland a few years ago and seem to have settled into their surroundings. One amusing sight was the electric fans in the cowshed to keep them cool in the hot weather! Some people don't have it so good!

Miscellany

During the year, there have been a variety of outside activities to keep us busy—weddings, hospital openings, visitors from England, Papua and other parts of India coming to see our work in this area; Summer Schools for the villagers, Adult Literacy Classes for the women, Retreats for the Presbyters and their wives, etc.

Future

Pat Roberts and Gwen Morris retire this year and Eileen Butterfield is going on furlough and then leaving this Diocese to become Warden of Vishranthi Nilayam in Bangalore on her return. Several ministers are retiring, and there is a great shortage of leaders in the church for the various works in which we are involved. Rev. L.V. Azariah has been appointed Treasurer of the Diocese, and for this, we are glad as it is time Indian people were being trained to take up these important jobs. His taking up this work leaves us without a Divisional Chairman, and this too is equally important. In Women's Work, also we have to rethink and plan for the future of work among women in the Diocese, as leaders are so few. With the financial help of Kindernothilfe, we can now have full-time wardens for our hostels but these people need careful selection and training.

We need more money, preferably from within India, but also donations from overseas, in order to pay a living wage to the people we need for these posts of responsibility. We need the right people both from India and overseas. Many people want to see the end of missionaries in India, but just as many desire to have missionaries work with them as they take these steps of responsibility. We need the support and prayers of all so that we may be given the guidance and the strength to do the work we are being asked to do.

I am very conscious of all the prayers of fellow workers and friends both here and throughout the world as I am doing the 'impossible' at present.

Thanks

Many thanks to all who continue to write to me in spite of my not answering. Magazines, newspapers, books, food parcels, and old Christmas cards have been gratefully appreciated by me and the others who have shared them. Nothing is wasted and everything has more uses than one thinks of at first! Brings me back to the handkerchief tale!

Betty.

(Answer to the bird question: At the sound of the shotgun, the rest would all fly away!)

Letter 9
Furlough. Hospital in London.
Adult Literacy and Health Work

Dunfermline
31 December 1971

Deep peace of the running wave to you.
Deep peace of the flowing air to you.
Deep peace of the quiet earth to you.
Deep peace of the shining stars to you.
Deep peace of the Son of Peace to you.

Dear Friends,

A guid New Year to ane an' a'. As you can see, I am back in bonnie Scotland after a few setbacks on the way. In September, just as I was packing up to leave India on furlough, I found myself in hospital with suspected typhoid. Dates had to be postponed and on the new date of departure, I found myself in hospital in Madras with acute pain in the kidney region. Plans had to be changed. Instead of visiting friends in Switzerland and Germany on the way home, I flew straight from Madras to London and had three weeks in Mildmay Mission Hospital, London, while investigations were made. A kidney infection as well as an extra kidney were diagnosed! This period in hospital proved to be a blessing in disguise. I had the chance to rest after the previous months of tension, and let me get reorientated to climate and other changes. I am full of praise for the care and attention shown in Mildmay Mission Hospital. They proved themselves to practise what they preached. Each day began and ended with ward prayers. The staff cared for their patients as individuals, spending time explaining treatments, reassuring the anxious, listening to problems, removing worries and caring for the 'whole' person.

The sunshine was out to greet me when I arrived in London on 23 October. I had no sooner crossed the border than frost and snow put in an appearance and made me rush to buy warm clothing. Fortunately, this burst of cold weather did not last long and there have been mild, sunny days since, though the forecast for next month shows wintry weather ahead. I will be attending a missionary conference at High Leigh on 12 January, then begin a deputation in Essex on 31 January. I hope wintry conditions do not hinder me in my travels. I hope to meet as many of you as possible when I am on deputation in England and attending various courses and conferences. My provisional dates and plans are as follows:

January 21–February 8	Essex
February 14–18	Audio Visual Aids Course, London
March 10–28	Derbyshire
April 7–25	Hants
June 23–July 11	Lincs
August 28–September 23	Literacy Course, Surrey

I also hope to visit a few Scottish churches, though official deputation is over for now, as well as attending the Scottish Congregational Assembly 4–7 May. I expect to be on furlough in Britain until October 1972.

Now to fill in some of the gaps since I last wrote a circular letter. This was away back in February during the Post Office strike. With Peggy Hawkings being on furlough in England until June I was kept busy during the year camping with two groups of Bible Women and arranging summer schools for the women of the villages in three centres. We were glad to have Eileen Jacob (nee Bending) as one of our speakers and Peggy was back in time to join us. Our annual adult literacy course attracted as many as ever and book-selling continues to do well in our camp visits.

There are many new avenues we can explore in our literature work and we tried two during the year. Once we went by jeep along the main road for about 20 miles, stopping at every village through which we had to pass. Rather like the ice-cream man's "Stop me and buy one!" As soon as we stopped and opened up the jeep doors and set out our display stands, children and their elders surrounded us. Some came only to stare and laugh at first but we did quite well with sales. A Hindu primary school was by the roadside and the headmaster welcomed us into the classrooms to sell our books. When we stopped at a village square, there were other travelling salesmen to compete with us. They were making children's toys from paper, clay and twine—fish and mice with moveable parts. We exchanged some samples and I bought some of the toys for my nieces. In the next village, the children there saw the toys and wanted to buy them from us! We agreed, and replenished my stock on the return journey at the same time recommending that the vendors pay that village a visit as we could guarantee them sales! Another time we set up a shop on the veranda of our bungalow in Cuddapah and sold books to the school children every day for a week. With 2,000 children attending this school, we had many sales and we hope that through these our literature is entering Hindu and Muslim homes as well as the homes of our Christians. The Hindus and Muslims have the money to spend, but even the poor are sacrificing their daily sweetmeats in order to have money to buy books.

Our village medical work also continues to increase and our methods are improving. We have now progressed from handing out our pills wrapped up in the page of an old railway timetable or in old envelopes, to have them made up in plastic bags ready for sale. Visitors to our bungalow often find themselves helping us count out pills into monthly supplies or enough for a course etc. and clipping the bags. During this year, we had gift supplies of medicines from America, and this has helped us considerably. (*Reading this now in 2020, I realise we should NOT have been using plastic bags to add pollution to the countryside when disposed of!*)

Animal shaped vitamin pills were a great attraction to the children and we had to insist that only one tablet should be taken each day. Scorpion stings still crop up in almost every camp and in Cuddapah. The patients usually come crying to us at mealtimes or in the middle of the night. 11:30 pm is a favourite time. Many call us from far and near to come and treat their stings—most often to the foot or hand. The poison quickly shoots up to the top of the limb. There we are dancing around with the patient, shaking the limp to encourage the poison to come down.

We have had our share of calamities with the jeep. Twice we were stuck in the mud on the way to a village. The efforts of all the villagers and passers-by to get us back on to dry ground provided good entertainment! Another time the clutch broke and we tried to push the jeep along the quiet country road to the next town. When we came to a hump-backed bridge, we had to give up as the combined efforts of two Bible Women, Jeevaiah, Eliah the driver and I were not enough to get it over the hump. When we thought we had better prepare to sleep by the roadside (9 pm), along rumbled a lorry with villagers going to the late cinema show. They got busy with a towrope, and after many stops and starts as the old the rope gave way and had to be retied, we eventually reached civilisation.

In April and May, I enjoyed a respite from the heat (though not from accounts work as I took a trunkful with me). This time, I joined the Martin family in Ootacamund in the Nilgiris and enjoyed the hilly countryside there. These hills are not quite as high as Kodaikanal and so the cold was not too severe. The gardens of our home 'Ananda Ashram' were a mass of flowers and we enjoyed their fragrance and the wood fires with pinecones and bracken.

This has been a year of farewells. Pat Roberts retired in February and left on a tour of England before returning to India to pack up and settle in her native Australia but instead, retired to a house in Ootacamund. Eileen Butterfield gave up being Treasurer of the Diocese to go on furlough. She returns to become Assistant Warden of Vishranthi Nilayam in Bangalore. In her place, one of our divisional ministers has been appointed as Treasurer. He took over in April just as the roof was being taken off the office. He spent several months in temporary quarters in a classroom. New brooms are reported to sweep clean but this was taking it a bit too far. Actually, the roof was being lowered, not raised, as the building was in danger of collapsing under the weight. Another missionary colleague, Gwen Morris, retired in August to settle in London. We shall miss them all as co-workers in the diocese and hope that new missionaries may come forward to share the load of those who are left and share in the work of training Indian colleagues to take responsibility in the Church of South India. I shall be very happy to give more information to any who feel interested in offering their services to the church overseas.

Our next-door neighbours at St Antony's Industrial Training Centre also bade farewell to their two VSO's from England. We enjoyed their company and visits during their year in Cuddapah. Our hostel boys and teams from St Antony's had friendly football matches from time to time and appreciated the competition. Then it was my turn to be farewelled, and this brings me back to the start of my letter and all the postponements before I finally reached Dunfermline on 12 November.

It has been good to see the family again, especially my two nieces, Fiona seven and a half years of age and Heather five, born as I was on the way to India. They are a lively pair and Christmas with them was hectic.

During my five years in India, I have been very grateful to my friend Grace Dunlop for duplicating these circular letters and sending them out for me. The cartoons and sketches have been the work of another friend, Margaret Ford and I would like to thank her too for highlighting them. Over the years, my list of names has grown and I am sure that some addresses have changed. I think now is the time to do some pruning and to get this list more up-to-date so I would be very glad to hear from all of you who receive this letter so I may start afresh. Some of you have written to me in India and I have been glad to hear your news of work and family. Many thanks to all who have written, sent magazines and parcels.

Betty

Letter 10
Deputation in the UK and Holidays

Dunfermline, Scotland
10 October 1972

Dear Friends,

My year's furlough is almost up and what a year it has been! Travelling the length and breadth of Britain—not quite, but it felt like it at times—meeting new people, making new friends, catching up with old friends, seeing new places and trying to take it all in. Now, my sights are set on India again. I fly on a BOAC charter flight from London to Delhi on Sunday, 29 October, and arrive in India the following morning. I shall be going to Cuddapah first of all for a reunion with colleagues and villagers, then shortly after will move to the new district to which I have been appointed. I shall be working with a group of Bible Women and visiting nearby villages. It is also planned to start a second Children's New Life Centre in this area and I shall be involved in this also. My address from November will be Sevananda Kendra, Nandikotkur, Kurnool District, Andhra Pradesh. This is about 100 miles north of Cuddapah, but as Cuddapah is the diocesan headquarters where many diocesan meetings are held, I expect to visit there frequently, especially as Peggy Hawkings will continue to be in my old home. I am looking forward to working in this new district but shall miss all the villages in Cuddapah district in which I worked for 3½ years. Margaret Cragg, who retired from Cuddapah in 1968 after 22 years working in this area, is travelling back to India with me for a three-month holiday, so there will be great reunions when the villagers meet her again.

Well, deputation was quite an experience, and I learnt a lot from it, visiting churches and getting to know the people and hearing something of what the church is doing in its local area as well as in other parts of the world. My travels took me from small rural congregations to large town churches, from ancient historical buildings to a variety of modern architecture, from energetic, alive groups through various stages to the almost dead. I learned something from them all. I hope that they too learned something from my being with them as I tried to share with them first-hand experiences of village life in the Church of South India. The places I visited on deputation are too numerous to mention them all. But let me assure all those whom I visited that I shall not forget you in a hurry. I have some memory of each place; driving through a snowstorm in Tiptree, Essex; Mother's Day Service in Tintwistle in March where the building was so cold because of a faulty boiler and the whole congregation were on their feet doing an action chorus to warm us up a bit; being in Lincoln as the Cathedral there celebrated its 900th anniversary as does the Abbey of Dunfermline, my home town; and so on.

I have memories of youth clubs and house groups, Sunday Schools and district meetings, communion services and women's meetings. It was a wonderful surprise too to find that the Isle of Wight and the Channel Islands were part of the Hampshire district. So pleasant sails and flights were added to my more usual methods of travel by bus, train and car. The Isle of Wight in springtime was a lovely sight and I managed to see much of the island as I visited most of the Congregational Churches there. I met a doctor from Ceylon, now a Medical Officer at the prison, and heard some of his experiences there. While on the Island I began to realise that even the small stretch of water, which separates it from the mainland really cuts it off, especially during bad storms or strikes, and the islands are different from the 'overners' from over the water. The ministers have a very thriving Fraternal and I appreciated being able to share in their monthly meeting. In Basingstoke District, my memory is of Tadley Church with the pulpit and gallery set so high that I felt I should disappear through the roof when I stood up!

Taking part in the Hampshire Spring Assembly in Southampton and passing on the Kiss of Peace round the assembly brought a link with the Church of South India. My most vivid memory of Jersey is the crowded gathering in a house, when sitting on the stairs, on the floor in every room of the house and in the hallway, groups did Bible Study Indian style, i.e. only one person in each group was allowed to read the Bible. (In Andhra Pradesh, only 21 per cent are literate.) The rest of our gathering was 'illiterate' for the time being. After discussing a passage, the group were to discuss how they would put on a modern play on the theme and as there wasn't time to perform it, were to give a report as it would appear in the newspaper after the drama. The results made everyone think, and I am sure many had never experienced such a Bible Study like this before.

Then off to Guernsey in a little 10-seater plane in the loveliest flight I have ever had. Then to join my next hosts—a family of horticulturalists busy with their harvests of freesias and roses. Helping in the process of bunching, wrapping in cotton wool and inserting into plastic sleeves, I learned a little about the hard life of an islander and the rush to get flowers ready for the next morning's plane in order to catch the market.

I was so grateful in all my travels for the way people welcomed me into their homes and in many cases treated me as one of the family. I came to learn so much about my various hosts and their families, and sometimes to share in some of their problems and difficulties. I felt that a few were a bit apprehensive beforehand about what kind of queer person a missionary was and what they would say to her, or feed her on, till they found out that I wasn't anything out of the ordinary and ate just as they did and was ready to try out their local dishes. The delicacy, which I will best remember of my deputation experiences, is eating spider crab straight from the shell. With nutcrackers in one hand to crack open the shell, and bread and butter in the other, using fingers to pick out the fleshy meat, I tucked in as heartily as the others did. It won't be long till I am back in India eating rice and curry with my fingers"!

Though I missed official deputation in Scotland, I was able to visit several congregations and speak at meetings, as well as attend the Scottish Congregational Union Assembly in May. Churches included Baptist and Church of Scotland, as well as Congregational, I also attended various courses. Although I was homesick for India after being back in Britain only a few weeks, a year passes all too quickly when so many activities are packed into it. All the courses were very worthwhile and have given me much food for thought. The audio-visual courses at the Methodist Missionary Headquarters provided me with useful tips for deputation work as well as for village work in India. Taking place during the electric power cuts, we were quite at home with pressure lamps and battery-operated projectors. We were not quite prepared for the lift, which stuck just short of the seventh floor when the current was not on full strength but had to wait to be rescued by the engineer and his hand winch. In village India, there are very few houses with more than one storey, and lifts are unheard of.

A Careers Conference at Alloa brought together young people who were shown different forms of service through talks and visits to Social Work

Departments, Police Headquarters and hospitals for the mentally handicapped. The St Andrew's Hall Reunion in Selly Oak gave me a chance to see the new buildings there, and to meet with new missionaries and those who have been retired for many years. At the reunion were several over 80 years of age who were some of the first students at Carey Hall, as well as some of the first St Andrew's Hall students from 1966. I was sorry to miss the CCWM Swanwick Conference but I had another spell in hospital at that time. This time, I had my appendix out and several piles removed in Mildmay Mission Hospital, London. Again, I appreciated the care and concern of all the staff there and was soon fit and well and able to attend a Summer Institute of Linguistics run by the Wycliffe Bible Translators in Stokenchurch, near High Wycombe. This was an excellent course and more than ever before did I learn how much I did not know about Indian culture and language! How I longed to have an Indian colleague beside me so that we could have worked on problems of teaching illiterate adults. Dr Sarah Gudschinsky was the main lecturer and we gained much from her worldwide experience of adult literacy.

It was not all work and no play during the year. I had a short holiday with my parents touring the North of Scotland by car over the Easter weekend. We worshipped in Canisbay Church, near John O'Groats on Easter Sunday. The Queen Mother's Castle of May home is nearby, and she comes to this church when she is on holiday there. On the way, we stopped to visit Crathie Kirk where the Queen and Royal Family worship when they are on holiday at the nearby Balmoral. In spite of all my travels in India and England, I appreciated the wild beauty of the North of Scotland, as we motored through Thurso and Tongue and down by Loch Ness. We were NOT responsible for the appearance of the 'hoax' Nessie monster that was fished out while we were there!

In May, I had a very enjoyable, restful holiday in Switzerland in a centre run by the World Council of Churches for church workers. There were 30 people from about 12 different countries including Finland, Hungary, Poland, Portugal and Yugoslavia and we had wonderful opportunities to share experiences of our different church work as well as enjoy the beauty of Switzerland. In spite of the variety of languages, there was a real sense of belonging one with the other, and of being members of the one family. On route to and from Locarno, I was able to visit some colleagues in India whose homes are in Germany and Holland. I was sorry that I could not include all those I had meant to visit on my original trip home from India. In my travels in England, I was able to meet some of the

V.S.O.'s who worked in Cuddapah, and also the families of Carey Hall friends, and catch up on news.

The end of my furlough period in Britain has been marked by attending the Church of South India 25th anniversary celebrated in St Paul's Cathedral on 24 September. This was a wonderful service, with many past and present missionaries joining with the Indians in giving thanks for this united church, which has done much to promote unity among other Churches throughout the world.

It was another thrill, as a member of the Church of South India, to be in at the beginning of the United Reformed Church (Congregational/Presbyterian) which was inaugurated on 5 October. Although I was there only as an observer and accommodated in the 'lesser hall', I yet felt part of the excitement as I joined with the thousands who queued to get into the Methodist Central Hall. The Thanksgiving Service in Westminster Abbey was relayed to those of us in the overflow in the St Margaret's Chapel next door and we joined in the celebrations just as fully there. Just as we in India are having talks with other Churches with a view to a larger Union, so this new U.R.C. is already scheduled to have a discussion with another Church. So the church grows as it is ever outward-looking.

Now I must leave Westminster and St Paul's, and return to the rural congregations of the Church of South India where some worship in mud huts or in shady corners. The buildings are not the important thing. The real Church is the people and in the villages of Rayalaseema, it is very much alive. I go back to share in the work of strengthening and building, encouraging and training, healing and teaching.

Many thanks to all who are praying for me as I prepare to return and start in a new district, and for those who have given me gifts for my work.

It has been grand to see so many of you during the year and I am only sorry that I have not been able to see you all. I look forward to hearing from you and shall try to keep you up-to-date with my doings this next term in India. Because of the cheaper charter flights and a new pattern of service and furlough, I expect to be home for a few months in the spring of 1975.

In the meantime, all good wishes for the Christmas Season—in case I am too busy to write again before then.

Betty

Letter 11
New Area – Transfer to Nandikotkur
Children's New Life Centre

Sevananda Nilayam, Nandikotkur

4 April 1973

Dear Friends,

Happy New Year! No, I'm not getting my seasons mixed up. Today is Ugadi, Telugu New Year's Day. At the same time, let me wish you a Happy Easter time, for it is not far away. Thinking of Easter and Spring makes me think of new things. I really feel that since my return from the furlough, I have been experiencing so many new things I must share some of them with you.

New address...new name...new colleagues...new job...

I was posted to a new area after my return. After living in a huge 'palace' in Cuddapah, built for the East India Company, I am now in a tiny little house 10 ft x 11 ft. I love my new abode and have it looking like home with some of my belongings here. Others I left in Cuddapah meantime. I like the compound very much. It is a real oasis in the midst of buildings—with our own little church, maternity hospital, houses and well.

In 1940, Sevananda Ashram was established here in Nandikotkur. Women lived together as a separate community and had common meals together, worked and worshipped together. As over the years the personnel and pattern changed slightly, a new name was decided on. We kept the first part—Seva (service) Ananda (joy) and added Nilayam instead of Ashram. This simply means 'dwelling place'. It has a deeper meaning to many as it is used in the Bible where GOD dwells in a place. Here we dwell in Sevananda Nilayam.

Who are we? Rachel from Kerala is a missionary like myself, but Indian. She comes from a different background, a State where there is a high percentage of literacy and Christianity. Dayamani is from North Andhra Pradesh. Rathnamma is here temporarily for a year to see if she is suited to the work. If satisfactory she will be sent for two years' Bible training. Sarojini is an auxiliary midwife who joined us on 1 April. She too is here for a period of testing, and she may prove to be the person to take over in the hospital from Nurse Elsie Prakashamma who will be 60 next week and due to retire. Manikyamma and Mariamma the Assistant Bible Women have had very little schooling but help both here and in camp in many ways. Rathnaswami is the gardener, waterman and general odd-job man. He lives with his wife Mariamma and their two sons Vijaya Raj and Sam on the compound. My cook Jeevaiah and his wife Mariamma, their two sons Prathap, Prabhakar and new daughter born on 11 January live on the compound.

We are quite a large family here at Sevananda Nilayam. We are expecting several additions. Rathnaswami's family expect a new baby soon, and I shall have responsibility for 20 boys and girls about 9 years of age, arriving at the beginning of June for our new Children's New Life Centre. The teacher-cum-warden Mr Rathnaswami has been appointed, and he and his wife will join us at the end of May.

New district: New Job

I have been camping in some of the villages in this area and finding how they compare or differ from Cuddapah District. Transport is by bus, bullock cart, horse and cart or by walk—no such luxury as a jeep here. The land is very flat and barren and stony in these parts. When the rains don't come no crops can be planted, so bare empty fields stretch for miles with hardly a tree in sight except round the villages. When the wind blows it carries with it the red dust until buildings, trees and people are covered in a fine film. One village is called Erramattam—(Telugu meaning Red Dust)—and aptly so. Where the main canal runs through the district, the fields are fruitful—with rice, other grains, groundnuts, tobacco, sunflowers (grown for seed, which is used for cooking oil), chillies, cotton, onions and other vegetables. Water is a great problem where there is no canal and this year because the rains did not come in time, the government and organisations like Oxfam are busy deepening wells, or boring new ones as fast as they can, to try to provide water before the really hot weather comes.

Some villagers in this area carry their water pots—two balanced on a bamboo pole over their shoulders, rather like scales. In most other places, the water is carried in clay, metal or brass water pots on the shoulder or hip.

Most of the Congregations in this area were formerly Anglican before joining the Church of South India, as the first missionaries were S.P.G. (Society for the Propagation of the Gospel). It is interesting to see the altar candles and cross (often a crucifix) in even the smallest mud hut, and in some a large processional cross. Some of the Anglican Churches did not join the Church of South India in 1947 and remain as a separate church. There are Roman Catholic and American Baptists also working in many of the villages. There are friendly relationships between all these groups and recently I was asked to speak at a Baptist Harvest Thanksgiving Service.

As well as visiting the villages with the Bible Women as I did in Cuddapah District, I am also helping in the hospital during deliveries. Recently, while the Bible Women were in camp and I was recovering from food poisoning (?) I was involved in several cases, which fast deepened my interest in midwifery. Five in a week was a record for our little two-bedded hospital. The cases ranged from the straightforward to the side of the head presentation, a mother with fits after delivery and a breech case, which was very difficult and the baby almost died. We have a very helpful Hindu doctor nearby who comes when we call him for any emergency, and he too said it was a miracle that the mother and son lived. All of us, including the Hindu mother, said it was only by God's grace they survived. The power of prayer in that room was equal to the best scientific equipment, which we did not have.

I am learning new customs, especially in the maternity line. Some are very like our 'old wives' tales, but great is people's belief in them. As soon as a mother gives birth, she has cotton wool put in her ears and a triangular piece of white cloth tied around her head like a scarf. This is to keep her from getting a chill. (In cold weather, the ears are the first thing to be wrapped up in a woollen scarf— though the hands and feet may be bare and very little other clothing worn!) The new mother is not allowed a bath until the third, fifth, seventh or ninth day. Until then she must eat a special diet, which is anything but nourishing for her and the new baby. On the auspicious day decided by her elders, she is given a ceremonial bath and then the baby has a cross scratched on his forehead with a red-hot needle, and a square scratched around his umbilical cord. These are to keep him from having fits or fatal diseases. (They do not always work!) The scratch often goes septic and is very painful. What the small child suffers through these old superstitions!. The baby is not given a name until his baptism that maybe anything from a month to several years. Until then he is called 'the little one' or 'baby'.

In our little chapel dedicated to St Francis of Assisi, we hold services three times a day when we take it in turn to lead. We have morning and evening prayers at 6:30 and a time of intercession at midday. Any visitors at these times join us. We worship in the village church on Sunday mornings and evenings and frequently the women's fellowship meets in our hall on a Sunday afternoon. Most of the women are teachers in the local schools.

When we are not camping in the villages or helping in the hospital we can still find plenty to do here. Recently, we have been selling books and Bibles in the market that takes place every Monday. This has been an interesting venture and we have inspired another bookshop to open up selling Hindi literature. Last week we went to the school attached to our church and sold small books and cards to the children every day during their morning interval. It was amazing how the response grew. Eager readers came back for more books and were eagerly recommending the best titles to their friends. Christmas cards sent by many friends in Britain have been cut to postcard size and a lyric printed on the back. Many children buy them for the picture and the latest craze is for glittery cards.

This week we visited another school—a Government one this time—and we were welcomed there with our wares and urged to come again. The Hindu Headmaster advised us to come before the bell rings so that the children can buy our books instead of spending their money on sweets and other eatables at the interval!

I have just been reading a book myself—*Pig in Paradise* by Elma M. Williams, in which she says… "sheeps is folks but pigs is people".

Just as she found pigs interesting, so I find people more and more interesting. So many anecdotes but no space to relate them all. Just a few reminiscences…

In one of the villages, a seven-year-old boy relived his Christmas experiences as he answered my question on how he had spent it. Like some of our Scots expressions, his Telugu could not be put into English, but his eyes widened, his face lit up and his whole body told of such excitement on Christmas Eve that he could not sleep. Joy for him was not the thought of a toy-filled stocking after Santa's visit, but new clothes, singing carols in a procession around the village in the starlight, a dawn service in the daily-decorated Church, and a feast on Christmas day—meat and sweets. There, by ourselves on the veranda of the church, the two of us talked together. Reminded me of a T.V. programme in Scotland where children were interviewed and asked a variety of questions. Both the cameraman and interviewer were experts at getting the best out of the children. Oh to have had my tape-recorder with me at 'my' interview!

I heard of another incident—this time of my niece Heather. At 6½ she is a bit afraid of the unnatural—fairies, Santa etc. Her imagination takes a bit of beating. After losing a tooth, she dared to put it below her pillow for the fairies to take away. When asked by her mother if she had heard the fairies, who had left her 5 p and taken away the tooth, without any hesitation she said, "No but I saw them. I only saw a half of them, and they were shiny silver!"

People are interesting. When I went with several Bible women and a group of village women who had come for a Retreat, to visit the ancient fort and buildings in the town, we learned that the Nawab—Muslim Ruler—was in residence for a few days to attend a Muslim festival. A local resident asked if we could meet the Nawab, and he graciously received us. Again, I say it—people are interesting! This Persian by birth, speaking perfect English, welcomed us into his reception room and we talked about a variety of things, including his education in Bishop Cotton Boys' School in Bangalore—one of our L.M.S. Institutions. His son is now studying there, and he regretfully added that attendance at morning prayers is not now compulsory for non-Christians as it was in his day. He says he appreciated all he learned there and commented on the similarity between the Muslim scriptures and the Bible. We both agreed that there should be more inter-mixing between the people of different faiths so that we can learn from each other and work with each other.

One villager's comments on our proposed visit to the fort—"What's to see there? Just some old buildings, which are falling down!" Afterwards many were touched by the kindness shown to us by the Nawab and a few people were heard to remark, "He's just like us!" My dreams often reflect my doings in a jumbled form and that night I dreamt I was having a long confab with our Queen and thought to myself, "She's just like us!"

So my experiences of new things could go on, but I must keep some for another time. Who knows—we may even have a new State when I next write.

Strikes are nothing new to us or you, and we have been having more than our share of these since I came back. Government hospital workers—doctors, nurses, pharmacists—the lot—on strike for three months; Government employees in a variety of Departments, including Post Office; Banks on strike or working alternate days only for several weeks; electricity power cuts daily for many months; buses and trains cancelled or running spasmodically. All these are in support of the bifurcation of Andhra Pradesh. No decision has been made by the Prime Minister as yet, but the intense agitation is slackening off though there are still daily reports of violence. There is a cartoon of Mrs Gandhi in the daily paper in a contemplative mood. "To B or not to B" (B for Bifurcation).

Parcels have been reaching me in spite of the strikes, though some have taken longer than usual. I am still enjoying new Christmas cards! Many thanks to all who have written to me since I returned, sent magazines, parcels of foodstuffs for me and the villagers, and old cards for our bookshop. All are very welcome indeed. With the temperature now over 100°F or 40°C, it is beginning to feel a bit warm. I look forward to a few weeks' holiday in the Palni Hills in South India at our mission station in Kodaikanal. I hope to go there on 25 April and will travel part of the way with Rachel as she goes home to Kerala in the very south of India.

Betty

Letter 12
Buffaloes and Maternity Work

Dunfermline
5 November 1974

Dear Friends,

Having just come back from a huge bonfire with flames shooting high, and bangers (both the edible and the noisy sorts) I feel just in the mood to write my circular letter. The Baptist congregation who arranged the entertainment took an offering for Bangladesh, and this made me think again of all my friends and colleagues in India starving at present. I was asked, "How would your children in India like this blaze?"—to which I replied, "They would be horrified at the waste of such good firewood as they can't spare wood to throw out like this." It is time I was back in India instead of spending 10–15 pence on a hamburger roll, the equivalent of a day's wage for my local field workers in Nandikotkur.

It has been lovely to be home for two months. I had little time to inform my family of my furlough, which had been brought forward from April/June 1975. I flew home from Bombay on 21 September and return there on 26 November. I have had no official engagements during this two month period but have enjoyed the chance to meet friends in various parts of Scotland and share news of my work.

While thinking what to write now, 'Bees' have been buzzing around in my head—the literary kind, not the honey variety. I left India with bougainvillea and other blooms blossoming in my garden, with butterflies flying around them and beetles scuttling to and fro. My black-haired, brown-skinned boarders were busy in their gardens too and have a variety of vegetables and flowers. In the church, there are many baptisms, blessings and benedictions, as well as meetings with local Brahmins and hearing their beliefs. I had visits to Bangalore, Bombay and

Beirut on the way home. Not forgetting Bangladesh and the hardships there, which are being brought to our notice in the newspapers and on television.

Now to elaborate a little on three 'Bs' which have taken up most of my time during the past year.

Bible Women. I continued to be in charge of a group of Bible Women who live beside me in Nandikotkur. There have been some transfers during the year and new candidates taken on for testing prior to going for Bible training. We have been camping in the villages, conducting services and Sunday School (not confined to Sundays but held on workdays too), treating wounds, bandaging bruises and advising on family planning. We have been selling books as we toured around and also on a Monday at our local market. There is a great demand for Bibles and hymnbooks and we cannot get enough supplies to keep us going. The new adult literacy primer, which was a revision of the previous one, was released in August at an Adult Literacy Symposium. Almost straight away, we had requests to start classes for men and women in the poorer quarters of Nandikotkur. Before I came away, we were conducting evening classes from Tuesday to Friday. There is such a thirst for literacy among Christians. The numbers grew too large for six of us to cope with but local literates came forward to teach and we found ourselves with teacher-training sessions as well.

Boarders. There are now 21 boys and 14 girls in our Children's New Life Centre. We have had our ups and downs, both with staff and pupils, but things are settling down now. Mr Samson and Mrs Rathnamma, the teachers/wardens, both give of their talents. Rathnamma specialises in handicrafts—clay, papier mache, eggshell, cornstalks etc. She has also been teaching the boys and girls how to patch their clothes. She has a fund of action songs and tribal dances that the children have been enjoying. Samson, as well as teaching the second-year class, has been concentrating on the hostel garden and there are 17 small allotments that are tended by pairs of children. He supervised the pupils as they pulled down an old outhouse and built a rabbit shed. They took great pride in their work as they carried the heavy stones from one part of the field to the other.

Our two buffaloes, PREMA (named by the Pilots) and KANTHA (Rotary Club) are doing well and the children take turns in looking after them. Prema has gone dry, and she was taken to the Government Vet for artificial insemination. After several unsuccessful shots, we were advised to starve her, as she was too fat! After all our care in feeding her up! We thought this was too drastic a measure so decided to leave things to nature and when the children went home for Dasara at the end of last month, Prema was going with them so that she might meet some suitable male buffalo! We are hoping for better results that way!

Baby rabbits are the latest addition to our family. In fact, they were brought to me as I sat on the bus in Nandikotkur at the start of my homeward journey! I acknowledged the gift and asked some of the children to install them in the newly completed rabbit house. We hope that they will multiply and provide us with additional meat for the boarders. Food costs are rising daily in India as elsewhere in the world, and we are trying, by all means, to supplement our daily rations, through our garden vegetables, buffalo milk and rabbit meat we hope in future.

My other boarders—the College girls in Kurnool—have grown in number during the year. We have moved to a larger rented house with eight rooms on the banks of the Tungabhadra River. We were pleased that one of the two B.A. students passed her first-year exams this year. Staff problems was one of the reasons for my coming early on furlough as April/June will be the end of the academic year, with exams and accounts to be audited and I should be there.

Babies. Our nurse in the Maternity Unit, Elsie Prakasham, retired on 31 December after many years of faithful service in our little hospital. We now have Mrs L. Christianamma, and she is very happy to be back in Nandikotkur where she was first trained as a Bible Woman. We continue to see miracles performed in our little theatre, and I have had a share in some of them, including driving a seriously ill mother-to-be into Kurnool Government Hospital, 18 miles away, for a caesarean operation.

Before looking forward to Christmas celebrations this year, I look back to last year's festivities. It was a new experience for me to be driving the jeep along the starlit country roads, taking the Minister and Bible Women to three congregations for Communion Services on Christmas Eve. When we reached the first church at 9 pm the congregation were still busy assembling the paper decorations. Everyone settled down when the last streamer was in place. The second one at midnight was having the church pillars painted so those who liked to have a lean on something during the service showed evidence of this on their clothing! The third one at 3 am had the band out to welcome us and music was broadcast by loudspeakers over the village. There was just time for 40 winks before the 7:30 am Christmas morning service in our Nandikotkur Church.

Now Christmas 1974 draws near. When I see the shops filling with expensive boxed toys, Christmas tree baubles and household bric-a-brac, I am glad I am going back to India where our way of life is closer to that of life in Palestine

2,000 years ago. Many of our homes are like the cattle shed where the Baby Jesus was born. Some of the splendid houses I have visited in Britain are too full of other things to have room for the Babe.

It has been good to be at home with the family and seeing friends and relations again, but I am glad to be going back to India on 26 November. My family there need me, and I need them.

Betty

Letter 13
Poultry and Rabbits

Nandikotkur
27 January 1976

Dear Friends,

This comes with greetings for 1976. My doings this past year come mostly in the D's. When I worked in the Youth Employment Service I had a motto—"DO IT NOW!" I feel this should be my aim for 1976!

DAIRY. Our buffaloes continue to do well—all four of them—Prema, Kantha, Kalpawali and Rani. We enjoy milk and yoghurt and buttermilk from our buffaloes. Prema gave birth to a male calf in July but he died after two months from worms. Fortunately, Prema continued to give a good supply of milk. Local Government Officials helped us to plant a special type of long grass for feeding the buffaloes. In the wet weather, this flourished, but now it is hard work to draw water from the well and keep the plants watered sufficiently. With gifts of money from friends, we soon hope to get an electric pump, which will make the work easier.

DEEP LITTER POULTRY. We were able to start a poultry unit, again through the help of the local Government who supplied the fowls at half price and are very helpful in advising us on their care. We have 10 hens and 1 cock—beautiful big black Austrolop birds. They are kept in deep litter (9 inches of rice husk) in a bamboo hut. On arrival in the compound, they were put in a temporary room and within an hour the first egg fell with a crash on the stone floor! Their hut was hurriedly finished and by evening we had four eggs lying in the husk. Daily since then, we have had 5–8 eggs so this is encouraging. Two dozen eggs have been hatched successfully so we hope to extend this side of our Children's New Life Centre activities. The children take it, in turn, to look after the poultry and we hope some may be given a Unit to take home when they leave after their

78

3-year course in April. We wake to the cock's crow that sounds about the same time as the Muslim call to prayer at 5 am!

There are now 29 boys and 21 girls in our Children's New Life Centre. Some are now studying fifth class school subjects and from January six of the senior girls are having tailoring classes in the afternoon. It is hoped that those who show aptitude will be able to have a further year's course in tailoring before returning home. Children's New Life Centres are proving to be the answer to the needs of rural India today, and we are being encouraged to open more such Centres. The work is interesting, exciting, challenging and rewarding. Today there is a great shortage of leaders in the villages and in the rural Churches. We hope that these children, as they grow up, will become the leaders of the future and help improve conditions in their villages.

DEATHS. Our rabbits thrived—we had three generations—and they were much loved by all. Sadly one morning a stray dog broke through a hole in the wire netting and we found all 12 dead! There was a deathly hush as we all gazed horror-stricken at the scene. For some days we were all conscious of our loss, as we had no takers for the banana skins, vegetable peelings and other food leftovers. I returned from camp to find a grave built for the dead rabbits alongside that of a former Minister who was buried in our compound.

Sudden deaths in the families of colleagues brought distress and desolation. The brother of one of our teachers disappeared just before his wedding, and his body was found three days later in a nearby well. The teenage brother of another colleague, upset after a family quarrel, lay down on the railway line and was killed by an express train. He was a student in our Secretarial Institute in Cuddapah, where he was doing well. The husband of a servant taking part in a drunken frenzy during a recent Muslim festival dropped dead during the celebrations. We all know John Donne's, "No man is an island entire of itself." He goes on to say something to the effect that "one man's death diminishes a part of me". We are all bound together, and in India, my family extends to the relations of all my colleagues and children's families. I too feel diminished.

FOLKS WHO '**DROPPED IN**' ON US. During the year we have had several visitors—three English medical students working in Jammalamadugu Hospital for a few weeks; Andrew Bulmer working on a housing project in Orissa State; and Grace Dunlop from Dunfermline. Their visits were all much enjoyed and appreciated by the children, staff, and myself. They all shared in some of our activities, each giving advice and encouragement, and opened my eyes to possible new developments. We remember Andrew and his talks on trees and the various fruit trees we planted shortly after his visit—limes, grapefruit, mango and pomegranate—are a constant reminder of him. In his housing project, families are encouraged to plant a tree for each member of the family. With 57 children and 12 adults, we have not yet achieved the target of one each! Grace brought various gifts for the children, including a football, and the children cleared the ground of stones and thorns to make a playing field. John Sedgewick is remembered for his making a bat and the game of rounders he taught.

DANCING AND DRAMA. Asirvadamma, our third teacher, who joined the staff in June, is a Physical Education teacher. As well as teaching games and sports she has developed various dance routines to be incorporated into our dramas and other entertainment programmes. All the best Indian films have singing and dancing as part of the story. Grace took a cine film of the children doing a dance about harvest, so now we are waiting to see who spots our talent! This year our Christmas drama had the shepherds and milkmaids doing a few routine steps. As usual, the children excelled in their drama. With 50 children in the hostel, we had a bigger choice of actors than previously.

DEPARTURES. In June, after 12 years as Bishop of the Rayalaseema Diocese, Rt. Rev. C.S. Sundaresan retired in order to start a Spiritual Life Centre to serve all the C.S.I. Dioceses.

DEVELOPMENTS. In July, our neighbouring C.N.I. Nandyal Diocese was accepted into the Church of South India. We look forward to growing together under our new Bishops yet to be elected to each of these Dioceses. Within five years, there will be reorganisation of the two dioceses and the work in Nandikotkur will most likely be transferred to Nandyal Diocese.

The year 1976 brings more opportunities for developing our Sevananda Nilayam Compound. We hope to extend our maternity hospital and have a well-baby clinic or daily crèche for under five-year-olds. One of our Bible women is now in training as a crèche nurse, and we hope that she will be able to take charge of this new work on her return.

DEPUTATION. Now, I look forward to coming to Britain during September/December this year. I hope to revisit some of those I met on my last furlough and give first-hand accounts of the work here.

There are many more D's too numerous to go into detail—ducks and dogs on the compound; dust and drenching as we camp in the heat or rainy season;

jeep dynamos that break down and various drivers on trial who land us in the ditch or stick in the middle of a river ...and so on.

Betty

Letter 14
Bishop's Consecration and
Four-Month Furlough

Dunfermline
5 December 1976

Dear Friends,

Christmas greetings to you all. I have not been dreaming of a 'White Christmas', but already the snowflakes have started falling in Scotland. I arrived in Dunfermline on 3 September just as the long hot summer was coming to an end. Rain soon followed, and we have since had fog, and now ice and snow. Furlough found me travelling far and wide these past few months, and I have made many new friends and renewed old acquaintances. I am sorry that I could not see all my old friends in Britain this time. My travels on official deputation and other visits took me from the Isle of Wight in the South to Shetland in the far North, seeing London, Birmingham, Nottingham, Liverpool, Glasgow, Lanarkshire, Edinburgh, Thurso and Orkney in between! Just as my modes of travel in India vary, so too here. I have travelled by bicycle and bus; train and plane; coach and car. Lately, I seem to have had a jinx on cars—a puncture, soft tyre, broken clutch, gearbox, universal joint—and one car had to be abandoned by the roadside in Orkney when the engine stopped running. I trust that it was able to move again! Let me hasten to add that I had nothing to do with the damage, nor was I driving the cars at the time of their mishaps! My last letter ended with a list of our Indian jeep's ailments, which included a broken dynamo, landing in a ditch and sticking in the mud. This brings me back to the news of India.

The following diary of events gives the main news of each month of 1976:

JANUARY

This was a month of Retreats. For the first, we played host to a group called the Fellowship of Professional Workers. This was a residential weekend lasting from Friday evening to Sunday tea, and we were asked to provide food at Rs. 12 (about 75 pence) per head for the whole weekend! It worried me at the time, as I had never had to budget for a set amount before—but we managed it with something like 2½ p left in credit at the end! Now seeing British food prices this would hardly cover one afternoon tea!

After surviving this Retreat, I was able to enjoy the gathering in Madras of our C.W.M. Missionary Fellowship. This Annual Meeting is a good chance to see our colleagues from other parts of south India and to share news of each other and former colleagues now in Britain and Australia.

FEBRUARY

Official Diocesan Meetings took up several days, then back to Madras for a course in a Lay Training Centre for women Church Workers. There was an opportunity to share experiences and to visit various centres in the city—a Social Worker and a Crèche in the slums; Government Remand Home for girls, and a Roman Catholic Centre, which catered for the needy—orphans, disabled, homeless and elderly.

MARCH

March saw us in Madras again on our Hostel Excursion. This was a real gala occasion as our children saw the sea for the first time. We left Nandikotkur by private bus at 9 pm and travelled through the night, with the children's singing eventually fading away as they dropped off to sleep on each other's knees, or shoulders, or stretched out on the floor below seats or in the passage. Apart from a few 'comfort' stops and a picnic breakfast beside a rice field, we travelled on and reached Madras by midday—a 16-hour journey! Great excitement when we reached the sea and all plunged in, though some were a bit more hesitant than others.

APRIL

The Bible Women working in the Rayalaseema Diocese had their Summer School in Secunderabad and Alir. At present, there are about 23 Bible Women working in groups or in pairs in villages in the diocese. This get-together gives them the chance to refresh themselves and to learn new songs and activities to pass on to their villages during the year. We went sightseeing in Hyderabad, our State Capital, then a time of quiet and study in a girls' hostel compound in Alir. Mrs Eileen Jacob (nee Bending) formerly a missionary village worker in Rayalaseema is now Matron of the Hostel, and she was equally pleased to meet her former colleagues as they were to see her again.

The end of the month saw us bid farewell to 20 of our children from the Children's New Life Centre. They were our first batch, who had come in June 1973. Two boys, Rathnaswami and Sikhamani, were being given the chance of further training in the Boys' Tailoring Centre in Gooty. After two years there, they should be able to earn their living as tailors in their villages. Eleven boys went for a short course on building and brick making. Six girls went for a shorter six months' basic course in tailoring, and Bhagyamma was returning to her village where she was given a buffalo that would provide her with milk that she could drink, or sell, or make into butter.

MAY

May is the hottest month in our area and a time for holidays. This year Muriel Harrison and I went north to Nainital in Uttar Pradesh. This hill resort is noted for its boating lake surrounded by seven peaks. We enjoyed climbing the hills and peaks around (8,500 ft. and more) with views of the snowy Himalayas in the distance. We visited the Taj Mahal in Agra on the way north and I enjoyed yet another look at this magnificent building. We found workmen perched on bamboo scaffolding trying to clean the white marble that is reported to be turning yellow. We also saw a pair of bulls pulling a lawnmower across the well-cared-for lawns in front of this famous edifice.

I returned from my holiday in time to attend the wedding of the Warden of the boys' hostel in Nandikotkur. This was a happy occasion when many of his colleagues from other hostels in the diocese came to wish him well.

Then a new term with new admissions to our Children's Centre. We missed the 20 'old stagers' who had left in April, but the new seniors soon took over the responsibilities and welcomed the newcomers. Mrs Lily Margaret joined us as an additional member of staff and Mrs Christiana Devamani helps in emergencies.

Our Annual three-week Adult Literacy Course for women was held in the Church Training Centre, Gooty. We had a concentrated course for new teachers for a few days before the teaching classes began, and all benefited from this. Games were played and simple dramas enacted in between the reading lessons.

AUGUST

I feel that this month should be printed in RED as we had a red-letter day on the 15 August as we celebrated the consecration of Rt. Rev. L.V. Azariah as Bishop of the Rayalaseema Diocese. The Moderator of the Church of South India and two other Bishops, along with many Presbyters and Church members from towns and villages attended the impressive, colourful service in Cuddapah, the diocesan Headquarters. I had gone to Bangalore on an excursion with the Kurnool hostel college girls and came dashing back to Cuddapah by car for the celebrations. Towards the end of the month, I spent a few days in Cuddapah helping Peggy Hawkings entertain Rev. Charles Meachin and 20 young people from the United Reformed Church in England who were visiting C.W.M. work in India. The rains started early this year, causing roadblocks, and making some rivers impassable, so their planned visit to the area had to be hurriedly rearranged. It involved wading across a river at one stage. However, this did not dampen their enthusiasm, and they encouraged us in our work. Their visit to the Youth Fellowship was a memorable occasion as young folk joined in a game of human noughts and crosses. The musical session ended with everyone walking hand in hand around the room as they sang to the accompaniment of guitars and drums.

SEPTEMBER/OCTOBER

And so to Scotland. After a few days at home with my family and a visit to the Edinburgh Festival Tattoo where a group of Ghurkhas took part in a display, I was off to attend the Congregational Union of Scotland Assembly in St Andrews.

Visits to relations, friends, former colleague, C.W.M. Livingstone House and former deputation contacts were fitted in between official Scottish deputation in Glasgow and Mid Lanark Districts.

NOVEMBER.

English deputation in Bucks., Beds. and Hants. introduced me to new Churches, both Congregational and U.R.C. School visits in both Scotland and England were very encouraging and the children showed great interest and asked a variety of questions. "Do you get chips in India?" "What time do you get up?" (5:30 am was not appealing to the questioner!) "Do you eat custard with your fingers?" (This after an explanation of how we eat rice and curry with fingers instead of a knife and fork.) An impromptu Bruce Forsyth 'Generation Game' (television series) produced great hilarity as young people each tried to don a sari after watching a demonstration. Instead of being draped gracefully around the body, the six yards of material took on the most ungraceful forms!

DECEMBER
Now December and Christmas with the family—and back to India for New Year.

These are just a few of my 'doings' during the year. Both in India and in Britain the days and months never seem long enough for all I want to do. This letter is not long enough for all I want to say—to record all the multifarious activities—camping in the villages, selling books and medicines, building haystacks, re-roofing houses, having extensions built, dropping the typewriter on my big toe etc.

Now 1977.

Although I returned to Nandikotkur at the end of December it was only to say goodbye as I have been asked to start another Children's New Life Centre in Muddanur, Cuddapah District. As well as the Children's Centre, there will be a crèche and a health centre with nurses from our Jammalamadugu Hospital doing community health work in the villages around. Bible Women too will be based there and will visit the villages, preaching, teaching and following up the children who leave the centre. A travelling library and bookshop are also envisaged. There will certainly be new opportunities and new challenges, and I look forward to this next term in India. At the same time, I feel sorry to be leaving Nandikotkur. I have enjoyed my time in Nandikotkur, although it has not been without disappointment and frustration, tension and worry. I feel the better of the experience and trust that those who have had dealings with us in Sevananda Nilayam have been helped.

On 3 January, I go to Vellore to take part in a two-month course on Christian counselling and group therapy that I hope will help me in my new work.

This is yet to come! Thanks to all who have continued to write to me during the year; those who have sent parcels of food, clothes, toys and Christmas cards, etc., and the many who have welcomed me into their homes and churches during my furlough. Thank you ALL for your interest and support.

Betty

C   Christmas Greetings to ALL, as I

H   Holiday at home—and do deputation,

R   Reading, relaxing and roving around—

I   Inland, and on islands,

S   Shetland, Orkney, Isle of Wight,

T   Travelling and touring;

M   Meeting and making new friends,

A   All making up to a happy furlough of

S   Services, sightseeing and socialising.

G   Goodbye, as I go back

R   Returning to India on 27 December

E   Exciting days ahead with

E   Extra responsibility

T   Training in counselling at Vellore

I   Interesting experiences ahead and

N   New challenge in another Children's Centre at

G   Grassroots level.

S   So, so long for now.

Letter 15
Circles. Muddanur and Rajasthan

St Christopher's New Life Centre
Muddanur, South India
20 November 1977

Dear Friends,

As I call this a circular Letter, it occurred to me, why not make it so!

This has been a year of circles, not 'getting nowhere' variety, but progressive circles. So my theme is going to be circles, rounds, rings. As I thought it out on my travels, so many things related to circles came to my mind...

Circular Tours

I've certainly done plenty of travelling this year. I arrived back in India on 31 December after my furlough in Britain, coming via Delhi, Bombay and Hyderabad. I slept through into the New Year as I recovered from my jet lag. Peggy Hawkings and Eileen Jacob came to meet me at Hyderabad airport and I went with Peggy to Cuddapah, then on to Vellore for the two months' Christian Counselling Course.

Sitting in Circles in C.C.C. while we discussed, counselled and were counselled and had group therapy. A circle is ideal for a group as everyone can see everyone else and there is no leader as such. Not only our faces could be seen but as we came to trust each other we let our inmost thoughts and fears be shared with others. In so doing we were helped to understand, accept and change what we felt we wanted to change. I found this course most worthwhile, and it has helped me personally as well as being a useful experience for my work. Now, others from the diocese are eager to go and participate, and one Warden is on the present Course. A few days ago, I met Margaret Howden from Kirkcaldy, Fife, who had just arrived in India and is enrolled for the Course in January/February 1978. Its fame has travelled far and wide.

Circles

Circles have centres, and in March, I came to Muddanur to be in charge of St Christopher's New Life Centre. This is similar to the Centre in Kamalapuram that Peggy and I initiated and started in 1970. Nandikotkur is where I worked for four years. Circles have a radius and St Christopher's Compound is the Centre to which children come from villages in a 5-mile radius. Our compound is actually situated at one corner of a crossroads. We started our Centre with 25 children from five villages. Later, we will increase to 60 children and eventually take children from 28 villages, all within five miles of Muddanur.

We have had our ups and downs and slowly staff and children are settling in. We have Hindus of various castes, Muslims and Christians. Jammalamadugu Hospital plans to do Community Health work and nurses will be based at Muddanur and go out to the villages for home deliveries and nutrition talks etc. The Bible Women will concentrate on women's meetings, adult literacy classes, library and book sales.

Danam and Moses look after the six acres of land in Muddanur and the children work with them in the fields and vegetable gardens. We have had a good variety of vegetables including brinjals (eggplants), onions, a type of spinach, ladies' fingers (in English 'okra'), and a variety of beans and cucumber family. The Forestry Department gave us five different kinds of trees and we planted 120 of these saplings on the paths leading to the houses and round the fields. Most have taken well and the present rains are making them shoot up. These are eucalyptus and various bright flowering trees that will bring colour and shade to the compound. We have been promised fruit trees later on. An organisation called 'Village Reconstruction Organisation' (V.R.O.) encourages community development.

Houses

We have completed the first simple village-style house for the children to live in. Eventually, we will have a circle of six houses with the children in 'families' doing their own cooking, having their own garden to grow their own vegetables. The house is built of stone slabs quarried nearby and a thatch roof. It looks very smart with whitewashed walls inside and out. The boys moved in on

1 November and are very happy there. They have a buffalo and calf in an extension at the back of the house that they are also responsible for. At present, they continue to have food in the hostel but are keen to start doing their own cooking. After three years in the New Life Centre, managing things for themselves, they will then be able to introduce what they have learned here in their own homes.

Pills

Pills and Patients—seven children were down with fever and malaria. Typhoid was also suspected, plus the usual run of coughs and colds. We have been having heavy rains and cyclones as well as monsoon weather. There are pools of water and mud everywhere. This is a good breeding ground for malarial mosquitoes!

Wells and Bores

More rings—though there are square wells too. Our two wells are round. We began blasting out the rock to deepen them in order to get more water. In spite of loud blasts when we all had to run for shelter, we did not seem to make much progress. We were told about a drilling company, and they came and advised us to put a bore 50 feet deep into the present big well in the field. At the time of their inspection, we had a visit from a Bishop and his wife, and she had water divining skills. Holding a gold chain and ring in her hand she walked slowly around the well, pausing in various places till the chain started to swing in circles. By counting the rounds, she could forecast the depth at which the spring could be reached. I wasn't there to witness the day-long drilling operation but the results were as predicted and now we have a plentiful supply of water—15 ft. of water in the well, compared to the previous 5 ft. Now, we have plenty of water to irrigate our six acres of fields.

More Centres

The concept of Children's New Life Centres is catching on and now the Church of North India is showing interest. We had a visit from a Pastor in Orissa, the State north of Andhra Pradesh. I paid a return visit to his area and saw the compound being set aside for the Centre. It is in the interior, up in the hills, and will cater for children from some of the hill tribes where there are no schools.

Now, we are expecting another visitor from Bihar, even further north, as they too are interested in seeing what we are doing. Many people in India today are concerned about the movement of the educated away from the villages, and the growing number of unemployed in the towns. They are ready to welcome training such as we offer in the Children's New Life Centres, which educates village people for village life.

Rabbits

When I first brought two baby rabbits to join our other two, the big ones objected and chased them around their temporary wooden box—round and round. Several nights the noise woke me up as I lay outside on the veranda beside them. Now, however, they have settled down and we have fenced in part of the veranda so that they can have more room to run around and we can watch their fun and games. As I write this, two boys have come back from the vet with one rabbit having had stitches in a wound inflicted by its mother! All is not as well as I had thought! Fluff is flying!

Rajasthani Dances

When I took part in an Adult Education Conference held in Udaipur, Rajasthan, in October, we visited an open-air theatre in the round. As we sat in the semi-circular steps of the theatre, between the acts we could look up into the star-studded sky and could see the galaxies so clear. Rajasthani dances involve twirling at great speed and the women's circular skirts opened out into perfect rounds. Another typical act involves the balancing of nine glasses of water on nine saucers on a tray on top of a steel tumbler on the dancer's head while he dances balancing on the edge of a large brass tray, which he bounces across the room. Very skilful!

Circular skirts

These skirts from Rajasthan are all the rage in India just now. Bedspreads have a circular pattern with rings of various designs and animals, and this material is cleverly cut to make a skirt with ever-increasing circles from the waist down to the hem. I have two skirts—one a wraparound which is apt to blow open, and another with a seam, which is safer!

Gold Rings

I was entrusted with collecting the Bishop's ring, which was being made by a goldsmith in Bangalore. It is heavy gold with sparkling amethyst. Bishop Azariah celebrated his first anniversary as Bishop in the Rayalaseema Diocese on 15 August, Independence Day. The ring was presented to him as a gift from the Diocese at our Diocesan Council Meeting held in Jammalamadugu in October. This is a gathering of representatives of all the Churches in the diocese, as well as all the Presbyters and their diocesan workers. The Council is held every two years when reports on the work are read and new committees are arranged, and plans are made for the coming two years.

New Bishop

Rt. Rev. P. John was consecrated as Bishop in Nandyal Diocese on 9 October in a ceremony in Madras, and on the following Sunday was enthroned in Nandyal Church. St Christopher's Home is supported by both the Rayalaseema Diocese and Nandyal Diocese so I have not only one Bishop but two to serve! Reminds me of my interview by the LMS Board when asked what a Scot thought of Bishops. Just as well I am not another Jenny Geddes!

Cakes

Jeevaiah my cook continues to make progress in learning new dishes and invents ingenious variations of his own. I carefully explained a new recipe for a chocolate cake, which requires the dry ingredients to be thrown together into a tin, then five circles scooped out, into which the liquid ingredients were carefully poured—vanilla, vinegar, egg etc. Then a cupful of water is added to the lot and the whole thing mixed together. Jeevaiah's comment on this careful step-by-step operation, then mixing it all up, was, "It's crazy! Why do all that?" Why, indeed! But the cake in the original recipe is called Crazy Wacky Cake! (American). Recently, I saw a similar recipe in an English magazine, and it was called Muddy Puddle Cake! Jeevaiah soon had the whole thing adapted and modified, and it tastes just as good!

Games of Skill

This year when on holiday in Kodaikanal, I was roped in to organise the games section of a fete in aid of animal welfare. The results were so good and everyone so enthusiastic that I was called on again the next week to include the same events in an international evening in aid of a crèche for poor Kodai children. We had lots of balls, circles, coins and hoops for people to try their skills. I did a round of the stalls and was kept fit bending and stretching to erect the pyramids of cans to be knocked down by tennis balls, retrieving lost ping-pong balls from behind the clown's mouth etc.

Christmas Cakes and Crowns

Christmas cakes and crowns and decoration baubles—and more circles, and this brings me round in a circle from last Christmas celebrated with my family in Scotland, to Christmas 1977 and my new orphan family at St Christopher's. When the Centre children go home for their Christmas holidays, the 12 orphan children still cared for by the Home here, will come from their hostels for the holidays. I look forward to sharing the festive season with them and also Peggy and Muriel Harrison who are joining us. Already Christmas cards are arriving (unexpectedly by air rather than by sea I suspect) and we have started practising carols and a Christmas drama.

Many thanks to all who have sent me their old Christmas cards during the year. We make good use of them in our weekly Sunday School attended by an average of 150 children—mostly Hindus. A text for them to learn is written on the card and given to each child to take home. Some cards are being sold, after being cut and printed, and this brings much-needed funds into the Diocese. Many thanks too to all those who have written during the year and sent gifts of money and kind. The Jersey and Scottish calendar for 1977 adorn my walls, while pages from 1976 calendars are pasted around the hostel walls and the new house to brighten things up.

All good wishes for the Christmas Season wherever you are—and for 1978.

Betty

The following P.S. to Betty's Newsletter was written on 28 November 1977 and gives news of the cyclone disaster in Andhra Pradesh.

Many of you will know of the cyclone disaster in Andhra Pradesh and the tragic loss of life and devastation. Millions are homeless and many still in danger. Thousands of dead bodies are lying rotting everywhere and bringing sources of disease; cholera is rampant; many people are becoming vegetarians because of the unknown source of meat supply. Trains are disrupted, electric poles and substations are submerged in water; many have lost all their possessions.

Rayalaseema is well inland and so only very slightly affected by the storm—heavy showers and gales—but nothing compared to the coastal area. We are involved here in raising money and other aid to send to the destitute and Mother Theresa has gone with her Sisters of Charity to help bury the dead and care for the dying. Our Bishop asked us to minimise spending on our Christmas celebrations and to send the money instead for relief work.

Betty

Letter 16
More Travel, Kerala, Kashmir and Wedding Plans

St Christopher's New Life Centre
St Andrew's Day
Muddanur
30 November 1978

Dear friends,

Last year in my circular letter, full of circles and rings, I was involved in collecting our new Bishop's ring from the jeweller. Today, I was at the receiving end, and a ring with an aquamarine stone and two white sapphires was placed on the fourth finger of my left hand by my fiancé Leslie Robinson. We were engaged in October and the wedding will take place in Gooty on 16 January 1979. Leslie is also a C.W.M. missionary from Scotland (Glasgow) and is Medical Superintendent in the C.S.I. Hospital, Chickballapur, Karnataka. We chose Gooty for the wedding as this was where I lived when I first came to India. Ann Marsden, who lives there, and Leslie are second cousins, so nice to have relations helping with wedding arrangements. Ann will be my Matron of Honour. The wedding will be at 11 am followed by a reception and lunch for all who attend—probably 600 or more! There is no chance of having a 'quiet' wedding in India! Busloads of children from the three New Life Centres in which I have worked will be coming, and the college girls from Kurnool Hostel, as I still keep in touch with them. All are excited! Bible Women, presbyters and other colleagues from far and near will be coming. Our annual C.W.M. Missionary Fellowship is planned for the day after the wedding, so all can attend the wedding.

After the wedding and honeymoon, we will go to Chickballapur and a reception will be held there on 26 January, Republic Day for the hospital staff and others who cannot get to Gooty. Part of me is sad to be leaving Muddanur and the Rayalaseema Diocese after twelve and a half years, and all my colleagues here. I am also looking forward to new experiences and new challenges in Karnataka Central Diocese. Chickballapur is 66 km north of Bangalore and is 3,000 ft. above sea level, so it is cooler than Muddanur. I have just finished reading Cecil Cutting's book, *Hot Surgery* that tells of Chickballapur Hospital and the work in the surrounding areas. I have been involved in simple medical work in the villages in the Rayalaseema Diocese over the years. No doubt I will soon find plenty to do in rural health work and roadside clinics run by the hospital.

In Muddanur, our community health work is making good progress. In April, Jammalamadugu Hospital started a weekly clinic on Wednesday afternoons in our compound. A doctor, pharmacist, nurse and clerk come and see patients from the surrounding villages. In September, a trained nurse, Sunanda, came to live at St Christopher's with her husband who does general maintenance work around the compound. He also acts as a second driver. The nurse visits a different village each morning and sells medicines, does First Aid and gives other treatment, conducts home deliveries etc. In November, our new diesel ambulance arrived. This was a gift from U.S.P.G.'s special appeal through their leaflet 'Saturday's Child' and Lent collections. Gleaming white, it has a red cross on the back and sides and flashing red light on the roof for emergencies. Inside there are two side seats, which fold to make room for a stretcher. Diesel costs one third of petrol so this is a great saving on our old petrol jeep. In spite of having two drivers, I am often at the wheel myself, and one night recently went racing off to Jammalamadugu with the red light flashing and a patient suffering from kerosene oil burns. As it was an accident case, we had to report to the Government Hospital and give a statement to the local magistrate before any treatment could be given in our hospital. The man was severely burned and died eight hours later.

Having negotiated the getting of this new ambulance through the various agencies that have helped us purchase it at concession rates, I was sorry not to be able to enjoy its comforts for village visits etc. longer. It has given me the idea, though, to suggest to friends who want to contribute to a wedding gift that Chickballapur Hospital could use such a vehicle for village clinics etc. As Leslie and I both have furnished our houses over the years we have most things we need. A gift of an ambulance would be very welcome to the hospital and we could benefit too by having trips to Bangalore when it would go for hospital stores or for servicing. I make this suggestion anyway. I am sure Grace Dunlop who sends out this letter for me would gladly receive any gifts earmarked for this and arrange for it to be sent to India.

In recent years, it has been the fashion to give the year a name or a theme. We have had the 'Year of Women', 'Adult Literacy', 1979 International Year of the child, 'Saturday's Child' (the theme taken from the rhyme on the day of one's birth—'Saturday's child works hard for his living.') Several people have been inspired to come and lend a hand at St Christopher's. Michael Stanning, a bank clerk from England, came in March for two months. Daily he could be seen clad in shorts and with old leather gloves on his hands, wielding a saw among the thorn bushes surrounding the compound. He has written the story of his experiences while in Muddanur and is selling copies at 25 p with proceeds going towards St Christopher's New Life Centre. The booklet is available from U.S.P.G., 15 Tufton Street, London, if any folks are interested in reading one man's impression of life in India.

Rev. Sebastian Charles, Canon at Westminster Abbey, visited us with his wife and four children, and they too made a great impression in our Centre, and in the neighbourhood. Their arrival in Muddanur was not without drama as they stepped off the train in pitch black at 5 am at what they understood was Muddanur platform but which turned out to be miles from the station. They walked through fields to the main road and eventually found their way to our compound while I waited at Muddanur station wondering what had happened to them!

Rev. Robin Sleigh also arrived unexpectedly and 'impossibly'! Recently he returned to India to work as an agriculturalist in North Karnataka Diocese and was visiting Rayalaseema and advising us on the agricultural side. The Bombay-Madras Express train does not stop at Muddanur station but continues to Yerraguntla 17 km away. Robin dropped a hint to me that he would be coming on the Express and if I had any 'pull' with the stationmaster, could I stop the train at Muddanur? I have NO say in stopping an express train—nor did I even get his letter as I was away at the time—but such is Robin's faith in my capabilities! that when the train slowed down near Muddanur he was ready at the door and jumped off when it stopped to let another train pass! Surprise all around when he arrived and announced he had come off the Express!

Rev. Charles Meachin brought another group of young people from the United Reformed Church in England. Jeevaiah, my cook, who only a few years ago would get flustered at the thought of preparing food for one visitor, now coped with 24 for tea, dinner and breakfast. Not satisfied with my suggestion of something easy to prepare beforehand like a hamburger in a roll for dinner, he produced meat pies decorated with pastry rosebuds and other ornamentations! Talk about 'red sails in the sunset'—as the girls bedded down on the veranda, 13 mosquito nets strung along in a row looked rather like billowing sails. The six-foot-tall young men camping on the warden's veranda and inside the small room, found themselves being strangled by mosquito net strings if they didn't bend far enough! The young people were a great hit with the children and staff and joined in various activities. They were ready to be taught Telugu by the children, who in turn were keen to learn English songs. 'If I were a butterfly' with actions and guitar accompaniment was a great success. After they toured areas where CWM Missionaries are at work, the group divided up and Jill came back to stay with us for a week and entered more deeply into our activities and routine. She was given a warm welcome and urged to return after her college studies.

Margot and William Cutting and their three children also paid a fleeting visit and later their son Alastair spent a night on his way to the North of Andhra Pradesh where he is working for a year before going to college. Margaret Howden from Kirkcaldy whom I mentioned in my last letter, returned to Muddanur in October to spend a few months with me, lending a hand in the New Life Centre and visiting Jammalamadugu Hospital. She will be here for the wedding so nice to have someone from near home to be an eyewitness and give details to my family. Caroline Christian from Nottingham is also with us now, though unfortunately, she flies back to England on 15 January, the day before the wedding. She had read about St Christopher's New Life Centre and was inspired to come and see for herself before going to college. Both Margaret and Caroline are working with the children on Christmas decorations and gifts and being generally useful.

St Christopher's has doubled in size this year with the second group of children joining in June. We now have 43 children and all have settled down happily after some initial coming and going. They are working well both in the classroom and out in the fields, looking after the buffaloes and rabbits. For a time, we had a baby deer that had been brought to us by a man who found it on the nearby hills. In spite of careful feeding from a bottle, it died after a few weeks. We later learned that the buffalo milk we had given was too rich and that goat's milk would have been better. We now know for another time! Our rabbit population increased and their hutch was moved from my veranda to a larger area. A pair was given to Gooty Boys' Hostel, and they flourish too. I read 'Watership Down' with great interest, being so intimately involved with rabbit rearing. One baby rabbit died after eating tomato plants, which had been sprayed with pesticide so for some time the children washed all the weeds and greens given to the rabbits! At breakfast, one morning a boy proudly showed a basket full of rabbit droppings, which he had collected after cleaning out the hutch. Visitors never know quite what to expect when they come and stay with me!

1978 has been a year of travel for me—from Kerala to Kashmir and many places in between. I paid my first visit to Kerala in January and attended the C.S.I. Synod meeting. There is a saying 'Kanyakumari to Kashmir—India is One'. But how different the countryside and the people. Each state is so different and each with a character of its own. I enjoyed being in Kerala and visiting some of the old LMS areas of work. The Synod meetings were dampened somewhat by the news of the death of Mrs Flora Samuel, wife of the C.S.I. Moderator. Both she and her husband had been badly burned in their car on 31 December and had been admitted to C.M.C. Hospital, Vellore. Samuel continues to make good progress.

In May, I paid a return visit to Kashmir and had a holiday on the same houseboat on the Dal Lake, Srinagar where I had spent my first holiday in 1967. The end was somewhat marred by my having a tooth abscess, which developed into a large painful gumboil. Then on the way to Madras to the dentist, I slipped down from the top bunk in the three-tier compartment of the train and badly sprained my arm. However, it takes more than that to put me out of action for long!

Travels and meetings also took me to Madhya Pradesh, Coimbatore, Madras and Bangalore as well as lots of travelling in the diocese. As I am also correspondent of the New Life Centre in Kamalapuram, 35 km from Muddanur, I often spend a few days there. I was able to buy a scooter with some of the proceeds from Saturday's Child project. Now, happily I can come and go between these two hostels and also Cuddapah, instead of spending hours waiting for buses and then finding myself in a local bus with an intended capacity of 52 but more like 152 squashed into it! Only a few nights ago I came scooting along the quiet country roads in the moonlight with the stars so clear above, and the trees dark outlines all around. It was lovely to be out in the wide-open spaces breathing in the crisp? (20°C) night air. I continue to travel around the district visiting the children when they are on holiday, and their families, and showing visitors around.

Miss Emily Wardle who started St Christopher's Home in 1940, died peacefully in June, just a few weeks before her 93rd birthday. Many of her first orphans were able to come to Muddanur for a service of remembrance and thanksgiving. There was a good reunion and much reminiscing about the past and sharing news of the present day. Now, there are twelve orphans who come 'home' to St Christopher's for school holidays. During the term, they are in other hostels in the diocese.

Advent and Christmas 1978—the end of another year and looking forward to 1979, with new experiences and new opportunities. I go forward knowing that God who has been with me in the past will continue to be with me in the future. From January, I will be at C.S.I. Hospital, Chickballapur, Kolar District, Karnataka.

Leslie and I are both due for furlough and hope we may come to Scotland in August/September 1979.

Betty.

Letter 17
Wedding and Move to C.S.I.
Hospital, Chickballapur

C.S.I. Hospital
Chickballapur, Karnataka
16 November 1979

Happiness is like a butterfly,
which when pursued, is always beyond our grasp,
but which quietly awaited,
may alight beside us.

Dear Friends,

The above quote is from some butterfly-decorated notepaper on which I was writing the other day. When Leslie saw it, he commented that our friends and relations will have to quietly wait until we alight beside them. Our planned furlough for the autumn of 1979 has been postponed until sometime in 1980—hence Leslie's remarks to all those enquiring after us!

Leslie was asking if I had a theme for my circular letter this year. Until he asked me, I had not thought of one, then the song *Getting to know you* came to mind. I keep humming it and a few snatches here and there come back to me. I feel it is appropriate as a theme anyway as I have been doing a lot of getting to know you since coming to Chickballapur in January.

Anthony our cook and his family

Anthony has been with Leslie since he came to Chickballapur in 1968, and he and his wife Mariamma and daughters take good care of us. Arita, one of his married daughters, who lives in the hospital compound, gave birth to a baby girl in April, and she and her son Francis aged two years, and the baby, are often in the house. Another daughter, Rajamma, came from Bangalore for her confinement in May and was delighted to have a baby boy after four girls, including twins. The twins came to see their baby brother and all stayed over for a month. We had quite a big family in the kitchen quarters over the months. Amala, the eldest unmarried daughter failed her 9th class exams so left school and has been helping with the cooking. Rosemary has just written her 10th class and wants to train as a nurse. Jayasheela is attending school and is in the 8th class. All three girls do Indian classical dancing and often take part in school or church functions. Raju, Anthony's youngest son aged 12, always seems to be in trouble somewhere or other. He does not appear to do very well in school and is much happier chasing monkeys with a catapult in the garden.

Hospital staff

Since I came, several doctors and nurses have left to take up work elsewhere, to set up their own clinics, or to go to government service or to Arabia where the salaries are higher. These many changes with no experienced replacements have been one of the reasons for delaying our furlough.

There have been constant changes in the office staff also, and I have been helping to get the accounts ready for audit. Leslie's office is situated in the centre of the hospital quadrangle, surrounded by lawns and flowering shrubs, including poinsettias now in full bloom for Christmas. The wards are in an open square around the office/theatre block. The office has a door and windows on three sides so I can see patients and staff as they come and go.

Patients

The hospital has 140 beds but recently the records showed 200 in-patients. The overflow lies on mattresses on the floor in the wards or corridors. Each patient has a relative who helps to look after him while he is in hospital, and cooks his meals etc. so the wards are full of people! Sometimes it is difficult to know who is the patient! In the children's wards, the mothers can be seen in the cot with their child, or both lying on the floor below the bed.

Many are in hospital for several weeks or months, and I have been getting to know some of these long-term patients. Some come from a long distance away to this hospital, which is the surgical centre for a big area. They speak a variety of languages but many understand Telugu, the language that I learned. Officially, Kanarese is the language of this State. The script is similar to Telugu so I am able to read and sing from the lyric songbooks although I do not always understand what I am singing!

Hospital Chapel

Every Sunday afternoon the hospital chapel is filled to capacity with patients and relatives for a short service conducted by the local pastor, lay preacher or visitor. Hindus, Muslims and Christians all come to the service, and usually, a group of young people from the church provide the music—guitar, harmonium, drums and tambourine. The Kanarese lyrics are very lively and are sung with great enthusiasm.

Every morning, prayers are held in the wards and the nurses have prayers in the Chapel before they start work. Now, we have started rehearsing for a Christmas drama. As the majority of people understand Telugu, the drama is in this language. It is interesting to see the various members of staff with their parts written out in the script they can read but speaking Telugu words. There can be no sharing of copies. One nurse from Kerala speaks very good Telugu (as the angel Gabriel) with herself the only one able to read the Malayalam script!

Local Church

About 80 families are members of the local Kanarese speaking C.S.I. congregation. As in Cuddapah where I worked before, one's sandals are taken off and left outside the church door. Men sit inside on the left-hand side of the church and women on the right. As in the former Congregational tradition, a communion service is held once a month. It is nice to be able to go to Bangalore occasionally for a service in English and to sit beside Leslie. He usually plays the organ for the services in Chickballapur unless there is some emergency in the hospital.

Bangalore

This big cosmopolitan 'Garden City' is 35 miles from Chickballapur. When I first came to India in 1966, I spent ten months there in the Theological College Language Department learning Telugu, so I came to know it quite well. It is a good shopping centre and occasionally we go to the theatre or a cinema. It is also the headquarters of the Karnataka Central Diocese so Leslie goes there to attend Medical Committees and other diocesan meetings from time to time.

Climate

As Chickballapur is 3,000 feet above sea level, the climate is much cooler than the Cuddapah district. Nandi Hills are seven miles from the hospital and are 4,800 feet high. A regular bus service goes to the top but there are also steps and paths up the hillside to a temple at the top. Several times, I have walked up to the top and down again!

Rural dispensary

Twice a week a team from the hospital goes out to take medical aid to the surrounding villages. On Fridays, the route goes around Nandi Hills and on Wednesdays, the ambulance goes down the steep ghat road to villages 3,000 feet below. I sometimes go with the doctor, nurse, clerk and hospital chaplain for these trips and sometimes drive the ambulance when we were without a driver. The present old petrol vehicle is on its last legs and sometimes we wonder if it will make it to the top of the ghat section after the 60-km trip.

The response to my suggestion in my last circular letter about friends contributing to a fund for a new diesel ambulance for the hospital instead of giving us any personal wedding gift has been tremendous. With promises of a few more donations still to come, we hope to place an order soon. We are very grateful to all who have helped with their gifts both large and small. As many of you will be experiencing an increase in petrol prices, so too we here in India have increasing costs, and we look forward to the cheaper diesel-run vehicle. The total amount donated towards the ambulance is at the time of writing £1,567.

Leprosy clinic

At present, there are about 2,000 leprosy patients registered here. These are divided into eight groups, with one group coming each Thursday to the hospital for renewal of prescriptions, examination of wounds and treatment. Many are severely handicapped, with deformed hands, feet and face. Some live as beggars as their families and society shun them. Some are eligible for a government pension of Rupees 40 (about £2.50) per month, which is all they have to support themselves.

Sabapathy, Leprosy Social Worker

Dressed in white handloom, cotton shirt and dhoti (cloth wrapped around the waist and tucked up between his legs) with a stick to help him along, Sabapathy reminds me of pictures and statues of Mahatma Gandhi I have seen in India. In his sixties and suffering from facial paralysis he is one of the most active members of the staff here. He goes out with the rural dispensary team and helps at the leprosy clinic in the hospital. For the rest of the week, he tramps around the villages giving out supplies of medicines to the leprosy patients. How he rejoiced the other week when a man with leprosy, after twelve years of coaxing by Sabapathy at last appeared for the doctor to examine him and to begin a course of treatment. Many are ashamed to admit that they have this now curable disease because of the social consequences and some are afraid. Last week a young college boy came to the office and showed two numb patches on his arm. He was afraid that the disease would affect his nerves and prevent him from writing.

Children's New Life Centres

I was sorry to leave the New Life Centres in Muddanur and Kamalapuram, and still keep in touch with them and hear news of all their doings. Now, this Diocese is considering starting its first New Life Centre in Kolar Gold Fields, 60 miles from Chickballapur. I was invited to visit the proposed site and give suggestions, and I look forward to watching its growth and development in this gold mining area. My first visit to the area reminded me of the coal bing area of Cowdenbeath and Lochgelly in Scotland, with pit machinery and pit bings dotting the landscape.

Peggy Hawkings

Just as I am getting to know new people and new places, so too Peggy with whom I worked in the Rayalaseema Diocese, is getting to know New Zealand where she retired in July. She has been able to buy a house in Kerikeri where her grandparents lived, and no doubt will soon get involved in the life of the community there.

Medical Students

In September, an English medical student, doing her elective period in another hospital in South India, came for the weekend and stayed for a week as she found such a variety of cases being treated and operated on. Now, we have another two girls from London staying with us for two months and getting involved in the hospital wards, theatre and outpatients, and rural dispensary work. It is good for them to see how serious ailments are treated with the minimum of equipment and to see for themselves many rare conditions only appearing in their textbooks.

Christmas in Chickballapur

A new experience is still awaiting me, but I can see myself being involved not only with the drama as I am already, but also in helping sort out and distribute items from gift parcels from the Scottish Doll Guild and others—dolls, soap, safety pins, shirts, clothes, coloured woollen vests and blankets etc. As in Rayalaseema, I am having used Christmas cards printed with Christmas carols and greetings. These will be sold in aid of the hospital. Other cards will be printed with a few simple words about the birth of Jesus and distributed to the patients and their relatives, and for Sabapathy to give out to his leprosy patients in the villages.

And so to 1980 and our first wedding anniversary on 16 January. I have just been rereading my last circular letter and realising that some of you will not have heard from me since then. I presume though that most of you will have heard that our wedding took place in Gooty, with Ann Marsden as Matron of Honour, and Robin Sleigh as Best Man. As well as a reception and lunch for about 400 after the service, another reception was held in Chickballapur on 26 January for the hospital staff and local well-wishers. Again about 400 sat down for a curry meal. About 50 at a time came into our bungalow for food, while we sat outside on the veranda and received gifts, garlands, and greetings from local friends whom I have been slowly getting to know during the year.

More snatches of my theme song come to mind as I draw to a close…

> Getting to know all about you
> Beautiful and new
> Things I'm learning about you,
> Day, by day.

Leslie and I have been doing this about each other during the past year.

As Leslie has not sent out a circular letter before, this will be coming to some of you for the first time. My friend Grace Dunlop has agreed to include some of

Leslie's friends on the mailing list. We are very grateful to her for duplicating this letter.

With all good wishes for the Christmas Season and the coming New Year and hoping to meet some of you when we are on furlough in Scotland.

Betty and Leslie

Letter 18
C.S.I. Church, Chickballapur Celebrates
88 years. Three Months Leave.
Leslie Adds News

Chickballapur

4 November 1980

A foreword:

This newsletter is mainly written
by Betty, and the words in CAPITALS
are comments by Leslie!

Dear Friends,

In India, it seems to be the season of festivals and fetes, feasts and fireworks. 1 November is celebrated as Karnataka Day—the anniversary of the time when the former state of Mysore was expanded to cover the larger area of the Kannada-speaking peoples to form Karnataka. It is a declared a public holiday. THERE ARE UMPTEEN EXCUSES FOR A PUBLIC HOLIDAY—ANYTHING FROM THE BIRTHDAY OF A GOD TO THE DEATH OF A STATESMAN, says Leslie, and is celebrated with great festivity everywhere. This year, we decided to have a fete in the hospital on 1 November. We had several stalls of eatables, as no function in India is complete without eats. There were a variety of games to test one's skill, and I had a handicrafts stall, which included remade Christmas cards. We had a good turnout and raised over Rs. 1,000 (about £55) for the hospital. NOT BAD, CONSIDERING THAT VERY LITTLE WAS DONE UNTIL THE DAY BEFORE!

While folks in Britain will be celebrating Guy Fawkes Day on 5 November, here in India we will have fireworks and oil lamps decorating our compound on

6 November for the Indian Festival of Light—Deepavali or Diwali, as it is called in some places.

This weekend has also been our Church Anniversary, celebrating 88 years since the first L.M.S. missionary came to Chickballapur and established a church. WILL THERE BE A MISSIONARY FOR THE CENTENARY? The present building has been in use for 48 years and now there is talk of raising funds to erect a larger building. A GOOD OLD-FASHIONED GOTHIC BUILDING IN THE PRESENT PLANS. Most Sundays there is a small overflow onto the veranda, which surrounds our oval-shaped church, and the congregation sit on mats spread out around the sides. On special occasions, there are as many outside as inside. Every Thursday we meet in the hospital chapel for an English singsong but with fewer nurses on the staff who understand English— AND CAN SING!—the numbers are not very great. We brought a new hymnbook—*Scripture Union Songs of Worship*—when we were on furlough and have been trying out some of the hymns. Some of the tunes are new to us but there are also some well-known airs with new words—Ye Banks and Braes; Dambusters March; Choral Symphony; Jerusalem etc. On Friday, we had a quartet with Leslie playing our new electric organ (brought from Cowdenbeath) on top of the old harmonium. On Saturday night, I found myself singing a solo and Sunday morning, Leslie joined Victoria (visiting Doctor) and myself to sing to the accompaniment of a tape recorder.

In our last circular letter (November 1979), we mentioned the possibility of our furlough and paying a fleeting visit to family and friends. As most of you know, we left Chickballapur on 25 February for twelve weeks in Britain. We were not able to see everyone—nor even to inform them that we were in the UK. WE MOVED ABOUT SO MUCH THAT IT WAS DIFFICULT TO TELL PEOPLE WHERE TO CONTACT US. This letter may be the first that some of you are hearing about our leave. Forgive us, please. We had a hectic but enjoyable time—meeting new relatives and making new friends all around. Our travels ranged from Montrose to Helensburgh to Thornhill in Scotland, with an outing to the Trossachs and a climb up Crieff Knock We crossed the Forth Road Bridge as well as Rail Bridge several times. We had a refreshing time at Churches House, Dunblane with the Cathedral standing out in the deep snow, which fell overnight while we were there. Our travels in England took us to Liverpool, Woking, Hove, Worthing and London. We had our base in Dean's Yard, Westminster Abbey, in the home of Canon and Mrs Sebastian Charles and family. ALL RIGHT IF YOU DON'T MIND THE TOMBS WHEN YOU COME HOME LATE!

We visited several churches and groups with whom we have been in touch over the years, and enjoyed the opportunity to bring people up to date with news of our doings—and in many cases—to say a personal word of thanks for contributions for our ambulance. This has now been ordered from the company in Bombay and we look forward to taking delivery. Unfortunately, there is a long waiting list and we are told that it may take six months before we can get it. The present ambulance grinds its way slowly up the steep ghat roads with a few shudders now and again. Hopefully, it will stay together until the new one comes. We are very grateful to all those who sent gifts, both large and small or who handed them over to us personally when we visited them.

However, all too soon, we were flying back to India, and even although we did seem to have timed our furlough for the best of the year's weather, we found 36 degrees in Bangalore rather on the hot side! When the rains came a few days later this cooled the temperature down, and it continued to rain off and on for several months. HOWEVER, WE ARE STILL OFFICIALLY A DROUGHT AREA AS THE RESERVOIRS ARE EMPTY. The rains brought floods and fevers and cholera scares. Recently, all the hospital staff and their families had cholera shots, as there were a few cases in the district. This timely action prevented an outbreak and no doubt saved many a life. One of our visiting medical students had bad dysentery during his stay with us, and this rather depressed him and us, as it curtailed his involvement in the hospital and prevented him from visiting the tourist spots.

We have had several visitors during the year—some coming for the day from Bangalore and others staying for a few days or longer. At present, we have Dr Victoria Karney from London spending six months on the staff, through the U.S.P.G. Experience Exchange Programme. She is busy learning Kannada in her off-duty hours so that she can speak with the patients and staff. IT IS GOOD TO HAVE SOMEONE FROM A LONDON HOSPITAL AS WE GET OUT OF DATE HERE.

Earlier in the letter, I mentioned feasts and we have had our share of these—both at the giving and receiving end. Our local pastor and the warden of the girls' hostel were married in February, and then in October, I returned to my former diocese and home in Muddanur to attend the engagement and wedding of the warden and agriculturalist—Neeraja and Jacob—and my former driver Silas and his bride. It was good to be back and see how the children in the Centre had grown, and to see the improvements in the compound. Leslie unfortunately could not take the time off to attend these functions (TOO BUSY WITH COMMITTEES AND SUB-COMMITTEES). He has tucked into other dinners on other occasions, ranging from sitting on the floor of a Hindu friend's house and eating a variety of sweet dishes appropriate to that particular Hindu festival; or at a Muslim home where they celebrated the end of Ramadan—their month of fasting—with chicken and mutton biryani and several sweets to follow. We had a western night out as we dined with our medical student on the 24th floor of Bangalore's skyscraper, and saw the lights of the city and the floodlit government buildings with the golden Ashoka lions atop the white-domed building.

We have also had our share of entertaining friends to dinner or preparing lunch and coffee for several Board Meetings during the year. Having curry, served buffet style, copes with the 18–20 who come for such meetings. Having recently discovered a milk co-operative just a short distance away, I can nip along on my bicycle either morning or evening and get as much milk as we need for coffee and yoghurt for the unexpected guests—or when the Board Meetings go on longer than planned and another cuppa is requested!

I continue to look after the accounts and typing Minutes and reports etc. in the office while Leslie looks after the fevered and frail in bed and in the operating theatre. During the year, one doctor has left and another is leaving this week. The long-awaited Paediatrician started work last month and we hope that he will build up the work in the children's clinic. My right-hand man in the office who was nicely beginning to take responsibility for all the accounts and records left for another job, giving only 24 hours' notice so this was a great blow. My temporary helping out seems to be prolonged indefinitely now. It is planned to appoint an Administrator with experience in hospital administration and his arrival should ease things all around. We had some disturbing and unpleasant moments during the year but we hope for smoother sailing in the days ahead.

We have had our share of fun and frolics too. One acquisition during the year—a wedding anniversary present—was a swinging basket chair! There are several hooks outside—one in a mango tree to which it can be fixed. Inside, with our 30-ft.-high ceiling it was quite a feat to get a rope slung up over a beam from which we could attach the chair. With a large padded cushion inside, it makes a comfortable seat, though I feel rather like a bird in a cage. (NO COMMENT!)

The chair has to be moved inside when not being used, as otherwise one of the many monkeys, which roam our garden, takes possession. Then there is more fun and frolics.

And so to the festival of Christmas—not far ahead. Already we have started practising carols, and no doubt we will have a mixture of the old faithful as well as new ones with catchy tunes to sing as we go round the wards and visit the families of the hospital staff on Christmas day.

Finally, many thanks to all who have written during the year and apologies to those who are still awaiting a reply. MY FRIENDS KNOW BETTER THAN WAIT! We enjoy hearing from you and hope that you will keep in touch.

Betty and Leslie

Letter 19
New Ambulance

Chickballapur
20 February 1981

Dear Friends,

Yesterday was truly a red-letter day for us. Our new ambulance arrived. We had had a letter from the manufacturers in Bombay acknowledging the order and stating that the expected date of delivery would be May 1981. Suddenly, to get word on 18 February that it was awaiting collection in Bangalore was a wonderful surprise.

We want to write and let all of you who contributed to the ambulance know of its safe arrival. Later, we hope to take pictures of the ambulance in action—but in the meantime, this unillustrated letter comes to let you know the good news.

We would like to thank you all for your contributions, which have made this possible. We had gifts from many parts of the world—Austria, Denmark, Australia, India, Shetland, Scotland and England. From places as far apart as the Shetland Islands and the Isle of Wight, Liverpool and Colchester, Glasgow and London—and many more besides. We had contributions from individuals and groups; churches—Congregational, Baptist, Church of Scotland, Church of England, Churches of Christ; Women's Guilds, Sunday Schools and Pilots; Rotary Club and Old Tyme Dancing Club. Some groups organised entertainment and exhibitions. One group of young people had a Fill the Matchbox sponsored competition and raised £441. Another group made a wooden model of the ambulance and collected contributions in this. There were slide shows, garden fetes, house groups, carol singing as well as individual wedding gifts. We have had many letters telling us of the various means of raising money, and it has been a great thrill to us to know that so many people wanted to have a share in the ambulance. We would like to thank you all—not only for the money, which made it possible but also for your interest and support for our work here in Chickballapur.

The new ambulance will be a great help in our work and will mean a great saving in running costs as well as being more comfortable than the present vehicle. Diesel is half the price of petrol and we expect to get 12–15 km per litre in the new ambulance compared to 5–6 in the old one. For those who are technically minded the ambulance is a four-wheel-drive diesel engine vehicle. The company recently introduced a Peugeot engine and we understand that the engine parts have come from France and are assembled in Bombay. The model we have purchased has one stretcher, which lies under the seats when not in use. We have a flashing light on top—no siren—for use when we have an emergency case to bring to the hospital. The body is gleaming white with a red cross painted on all three sides. We plan to have our name—C.S.I. Hospital, Chickballapur—painted on the sides—one side in English and one side in Kannada, the local language. It was suggested that we put 'Donated by…' but we explained that the list of contributors was too long for that! With the company changing over to the Peugeot engine the price almost doubled from the first quotation we had. With a few recent gifts, our total has now gone over £5,000 so this more than covers the cost of the ambulance. The extra money will enable us to buy some spares and equipment and go towards rebuilding the garage.

We would like to thank Grace Dunlop especially for acting as our Banker and Correspondent all this time. She willingly agreed to receive donations on our behalf and we know she has written and acknowledged all the gifts, as well as keeping us informed over the months. We have had to go through quite a lot of red tape to get the ambulance ordered and the money sent through the right channels etc. We are grateful to C.W.M. for acting as our donors and seeing to the payment for us.

22 February is known as Thinking Day in Guiding circles and on that day we are going to dedicate the ambulance and officially hand it over to the hospital. We will be thinking of all of you who had a share in our ambulance and giving thanks to God for this aid to our work.

We look forward to using our new ambulance for our twice-weekly rural dispensary trips when we cover 60 km on two different routes. The ambulance will also be used for bringing patients to the hospital or taking them home.

We will give you more news later in the year—but in the meantime THANK YOU ONE AND ALL.

Betty and Leslie

Letter 20
Visitors and Volunteers. Hospital Building Plans

Chickballapur
22 November 1981

Dear Friends,

Last week Karnataka State celebrated Tourist Week with some of the important buildings floodlit, and various exhibitions and displays in Bangalore and other cities in the State. I returned from Bangalore with some colourful advertisement posters that I thought we could use to decorate the outpatient hall in the hospital. Rereading the slogans at the foot, I decided that it might not be appropriate… "Be here when it happens."

We look back over 1981 and pick out some of the happenings since our last circular letter. I think the first eight letters of the alphabet highlight some of our most important events. As you could not be here, let us put you in the picture.

A for AMBULANCE. Our eagerly awaited diesel ambulance arrived in Bangalore on 19 February and has been well used since then. It has clocked up 12,000 km already and is proving a great boon for our twice-weekly rural dispensary clinics, bringing patients to and from the hospital, and for hospital purchases both locally and in Bangalore. We are very grateful to ALL who had a share in this wedding gift to us. On 22 February, the Chairman of the Hospital Board dedicated it and handed it over to the hospital. Prakash, our hospital driver, is very good and experienced and takes great pride in the new vehicle. I still occasionally act as a driver too and enjoy driving it. It runs smoothly and does not make the usual noise of a diesel engine. As Prakash says, "It is just like a car engine."

B is for BARRY ROBINSON, our Medical Student of the Year. We now have a regular stream of medical students from Britain spending their two months elective period in our hospital. They gain practical experience of a variety of diseases and operations not seen in their textbooks. Their stream of questions keeps the doctors on their toes, and they too are keen to ask about medical training in Britain and compare notes. Barry will be remembered not only for his help in the operation theatre and clinics but also for his practical help in brightening up the outpatient clinics. Wielding a paintbrush himself, he inspired others to work with him. His inspiration continues with Sundaramma, a ward cleaner, now full-time as a painter, going round the wards painting beds, lockers, screens and other furniture. Women were occasionally surprised to see the previously white-washed painter appear with stethoscope in hand to assist them in the Labour room!

C for COUNSELLING and COMMUNICATION. We had Dr K.C. Joseph, previously of the Christian Counselling Centre, Vellore, and now retired and living in Bangalore, conducting a series of sessions with our English-speaking staff. With practical exercises and sharing in twos, we were led to examine ourselves and see how we could change ourselves rather than try to change others. As we came to understand the mechanics of communication and how essential this is for personal relationships, as well as for the smooth running of the hospital, we found how easy it was for instructions to be misunderstood. With over six languages being spoken by the staff and patients, this need for communication to be clear is essential.

D is for DOCTORS. Once again, this has been a year of many changes in the staff. We were very sorry to lose Dr Victoria Karney who spent six months with us under the USPG Experience Exchange Programme. Learning the local language in her spare time, Victoria took her turn with the other doctors in doing night duty and seeing patients in the clinics and wards. During her time with us, a doctor couple left, and until now, we have not been able to get another couple, though two young men have joined the staff. Dr Victoria left in February, and it was August before another lady doctor could share the work with Dr Latha. Sadly, after only two months the new doctor left to be with her husband who was transferred to Poona. Once again, we are on the lookout for a lady doctor. Our Paediatrician left for a post in Iran in August and we have still not found a replacement for him. We also hope to revive the Ophthalmology Department in the hospital, as there is a need for an eye specialist in Chickballapur. At present, the nearest place where eyes are treated is Bangalore, 60 km away. No doubt, we will find difficulty in securing the services of a specialist.

Not only doctors but also other members of staff have been leaving for other posts—some with very little notice—especially those going abroad. There is a great demand for hospital staff in Saudi Arabia, Iran and other Arab countries. Short-term appointments with high salaries attract many Indians even although they have to produce large sums of money for the agents who arrange the appointments. Getting the necessary passports and visas takes time but when everything is cleared, they leave with very short notice. The hospital has a system of paying salary in lieu of notice and all, with the prospects of high salaries abroad, are ready to pay this. However, leaving within 24 hours does not help in the running of the hospital!

On 1 January 1981, a full-time administrator was appointed. On contract for a year, he has brought many new insights and suggestions during his year and has encouraged more members of staff to lead the daily morning service in the hospital chapel. However, he has not proved to be the kind of person we need—someone practical who can see to the smooth running of the hospital, take charge of building construction and repairs etc. At the Hospital Board meeting next month a decision has to be taken as to our next appointment.

Mrs Grace Rao was appointed as Nursing Superintendent from 1 November and with experience of a large hospital in Bombay, we look to her to improve the nursing side of the hospital work. She appears to be very practical and is having the coconut fibre mattresses re-covered and the stuffing cleaned etc. The new bedding on the newly painted cots has brightened up the wards considerably.

E for ENCEPHALITIS. In November/December 1979, there was an epidemic of encephalitis—or brain fever as it is called locally—in this area. Last year the usual few cases were admitted, but nothing out of the ordinary. However, since September this year, again the numbers have started to rise and the papers are full of the number of cases and fatalities. Once again, mostly young children are affected although we have also had a few young women admitted. Mosquitoes and heavy rains this year have meant plenty of water lying around as breeding grounds for the mosquitoes that carry the disease.

E is also for EXPANSION. During the year, we have been considering the future of the hospital. Started in 1913 many of the buildings are in need of repair and expansion to cope with the present services offered by the hospital. A survey of the present buildings has been done, and the future needs for new buildings and modernisation are being worked out as a Master Plan. There is a great need for more private wards, pharmacy, administration block, outpatients department and staff quarters.

F for FULTON FAMILY. We were happy that Leslie's sister Frances and her husband John and their two children Niall and Kirsten could come and spend three weeks with us in July this year. Their being here was both a joy and a help to us as we could share with them some of our frustrations and needs and queries as to "where do we go from here?"

In December, we look forward to a visit from another Frances, and her husband Sebastian Charles, Canon at Westminster Abbey. In our last letter, we mentioned having stayed with them in Dean's Yard, Westminster Abbey. They and their four children visited me in Muddanur in 1978, and it is good that on this return trip to India they can come to Chickballapur.

G is for GARAGE. Our old ambulance used to stand outside in all weathers after the garage had been partly demolished as it was unsafe. When our new ambulance arrived at first it was given temporary shelter under the portico of our bungalow until the garage could be rebuilt. With some of the money remaining from the gifts given specifically for the ambulance, and with other gifts given for the garage, we were able to reconstruct the garage that stands near our bungalow. We are grateful for all the gifts that enabled us to help the hospital in this way.

Another

G is for GOLDEN WEDDING. We send greetings to Cecil and Eleanor Cutting who celebrate their golden wedding on 7 December. Cecil was Medical Superintendent here for nearly 30 years, and we live in the house still known as 'Dr Cutting's Bungalow'. Cecil's book *Hot Surgery* written in 1962 gives good descriptions of the work and outreach of the hospital and makes good reading for our medical students and other visitors.

H is for HERE. As the tourist poster mentioned at the beginning of the letter stated, 'Be here when it happens'. We close wishing that many of you could be here in the hospital to share in the various happenings. It may be that some reading this could share in some way. Maybe there are some like Dr Victoria who could come and share in the work. No doubt there will be other medical students like our present Scotsman, Kenneth Robertson, who can bring some inspiration, as well as filling their rucksack with packets of tasty foodstuffs, which we miss!

HEALTH and HAPPINESS is our wish for all this Christmas season, and for the coming year.

I is for ME TOO! Though Betty has written this letter, as she does most of my correspondence, while I am busy with other things in the hospital, I, Leslie, have shared in it, and share in sending greetings to you all, and thanks for all your prayers and help during the year.

Betty and Leslie

Letter 21
New Church Building Plans

Chickballapur
1 February 1982

Dear Friends,

Proposed New Building Appeal

Chickballapur was established as a Head Station of the London Missionary Society in south India in 1892 and Mr Richard A. Hickling was appointed to it in the same year as the District Missionary. Mr Hickling was concerned with the physical as well as the spiritual needs of the people of this area. In spite of strong opposition to Christianity, which existed in the district in those early days, he saw to the establishing of a hospital as well as a church in the town. In 1909, the foundation stone of the hospital was laid and in 1910, the Chickballapur church building was started. The latter was situated in the heart of the town—on the National Highway now known as the Bangalore-Bellary Road. That site is now occupied by a medical store. Mr Hickling was the architect of the building and Rev. V. Virabhadrappa was the first pastor. The church was built on the main road so that the non-Christians could recognise the presence of a Christian group among them.

Later, in order to expand, this site was sold and the present church was built in 1932 in what is known as Old Post Office Road. It was called, 'John Winterbotham Memorial Hall' as the authorities would not give the necessary permission for a Christian church. Rev. Paul Daniel was the first minister of the church. The total membership then was not more than 50. Mr Hickling saw to the building of the church himself and the coloured glass window with a cross incorporated in the design. The iron girders used in the construction were specially brought from England.

Over the years, the congregation has grown to over 300 communicant members, and there is a need for a larger building. It is proposed to build this in the spacious compound adjoining the Medical Superintendent's bungalow, where the first mission bungalow stands.

As can be seen from the above short history the Christian church has made an impact on the lives of many in Chickballapur and we believe it will continue to do so. Many of you who will read this have been associated with the church in Chickballapur over the years and we approach you now to help with the construction of the proposed new building. A plan has been drawn up by the Pastorate committee at an estimated cost of Rs. 2 lakhs. The diocese will bear half of the cost and the Church must raise the other half. The diocese has given permission for an appeal to be made.

Therefore, we appeal to present members and friends and worthy citizens of Chickballapur and to many past members and friends scattered throughout India and abroad, and request you to contribute liberally. We welcome your gifts and your continued interest and support for the work and witness of the Church here in Chickballapur.

Yours sincerely,

Mr G. Jayakumar   Dr Mohan S. Prabhakar   Rev. P.K. Simon John
Treasurer   Secretary   Presbyter

The Church of South India, Karnataka Central Diocese

Rt. Rev. L. V. Azariah
Moderator's Commissary,

Diocesan Office, Bangalore
17 November 1980

Authorisation.

The Diocese has approved the scheme for the construction of a new church by the Chickballapur Pastorate. The total estimated cost is Rs. 200,000 of which the Pastorate will meet 50 per cent of the cost.

The Property Committee of the Diocese has resolved that the Pastorate should remit their share to the Diocese before undertaking the construction. I, therefore, appeal to all Pastorates, Institutions and individuals they may be approaching for donations to respond generously. Serially numbered receipts should be issued for all donations.

The congregation is at present worshipping in an old building that is inadequate for the growing congregation. There is no doubt that a new and enlarged building is a necessity for the Pastorate and I hope that this need will be fulfilled as early as possible.

Signed: L. V. Azariah
Bishop in Rayalaseema
and Moderator's Commissary
in Karnataka Central Diocese.

Letter 22
Hospital's 70th Anniversary. C.S.I.
Hospital, Channapatna. Mrs Gandhi

Chickballapur

6 March 1983

Dear Friends,

WE ALL NEED A HELPING HAND

This is the caption below a picture of a small child holding up both hands to grasp adult hands. We used this poster as the theme of our hospital's 70th Anniversary Celebrations last weekend. Caroline, one of our visiting medical students, illustrated another poster of our hospital needs, with drawings of a stethoscope, blood pressure apparatus, stretcher etc. Another poster of a thermometer showed the 'temperature rising' as it recorded the thousands of rupees we collected during the weeks leading up to the celebrations. The cash income has now reached Rs. 30,000, and we have had many other promises of money to come after the potato and grape harvests next month. Several have given gifts of equipment and two have promised to build single private wards alongside an earlier gift of a ward that is now up to roof level. Others with 'contacts' have said they will try to get us grants for a pharmacy building, and other essential extensions to our buildings. Things are looking up, although it has not been without hard work by many people. All our involvement in various ways these past few months is one of the reasons for the delay in sending out our annual letter, which usually went out around Christmas. We heard from Grace, our editor, printer, publisher etc. that she has been getting letters from some of you asking if we are all right, as there has been no news! Now to let you know what we have been getting up to since we last wrote in December 1981.

Leslie came back from a Diocesan Medical Committee in Bangalore in March 1982 and said that he had been asked to take charge of another hospital 70 miles from here—in addition to being Medical Superintendent here. This small 20-bedded hospital in Channapatna, 35 miles south-west of Bangalore (we are 35 miles north of Bangalore) was established about 70 years ago. It was formerly under the care of the C.S.I. Hospital, Bangalore as they were both started by the Church of England Zenana Missionary Society.

We went to Channapatna on 16 April 1982 when the charge was officially handed over to Leslie, and Betty stayed on while Leslie came back to Chickballapur to get necessary medicines and equipment to stock the hospital and get it into action again. Three nurses and several ward boys and cleaners and maintenance staff were there. Betty spent a busy weekend arranging for the whitewashing of the doctor's quarters and other staff quarters upstairs. A doctor came temporarily from Chickballapur for a few weeks until we appointed a doctor couple. Now, with a laboratory technician and pharmacist added to the staff, the hospital is running once again. At first, Leslie went once a week for a night and day to help get the various departments set up and records established. Betty went once a month to pay salaries and check on the accounts. Now, Dr Kundargi, our Ophthalmologist, goes on alternate weeks and has an eye clinic. It is hoped to use the hospital as the centre for Community Health work for the villages around. Dr Devdas has just returned from a tour of community health projects in Kerala and Tamil Nadu to gain experience as to how to set about doing a survey. Now, we are doing some mothering of Channapatna and hope that it won't be long before it can stand on its own feet. For the moment, it continues to need a helping hand.

After a series of adverts, a Business Manager was appointed in August 1982. Betty had been acting as a full-time accounts supervisor since January 1982 and had been involved in administrative work as well as the Medical Superintendent's Office, and the Channapatna Hospital Office. There was not much time to train up the new man before we went on home leave in September 1982, and so, on our return, she is still lending a helping hand.

We were able to get away for 2½ months (September to mid-November) and spent most of this in Scotland with our parents. Betty's father had a spell in hospital having two glaucoma operations. It was interesting to be involved in a Scottish hospital as relatives of a patient—a new angle from our usual involvement. We arrived home in time to attend the Annual Assembly of the

Congregational Union of Scotland in St Andrews and were able to meet representatives from most of the churches. The C.S.I. Day in London was an opportunity to meet up with former colleagues from India. We were not able to visit as many churches as we had hoped during this furlough—or even to contact friends to let them know that we were in the country. Apologies all around. We had hoped to get the telephone installed in Betty's parents' home in Dunfermline while we were on furlough but it was not actually fitted until the day after we left Scotland to return to India. In Chickballapur we have been waiting for a new board in the telephone exchange so that we could get a phone in the hospital. Eventually last month they gave us a temporary number for two months to tide us over the Anniversary Celebrations. We hope that before the two months are up they will have fitted up the new lines and we can keep our number. At present, it is Chickballapur 69—if any need to contact us in an emergency! The telephone was installed in the Medical Superintendent's Office and our hospital carpenter and his assistant have spent several days making an opening in the door, with a ledge for the telephone, so that other members of staff can answer the phone if the office is closed!

Helpful as it is to have a telephone, which saves waiting in the local post office for trunk calls to be booked etc.—an intercom between the different departments of the hospital would be even more useful. Much time is spent going from place to place to track down a paper or check a record or find a doctor in an emergency. Maybe some benefactor will come forward to install this as part of our 70th Anniversary Celebrations! With the visit next year of a computer programmer, we hope to explore the possibilities of a small computer, which could remove many of the monotonous calculations and simplify the record filing and stocks of medicines and other supplies.

On our return to Chickballapur in mid-November 1982, we were straight into preparations for Christmas, and arranging to receive four medical students. Our stream of medical students doing their two-month elective period continues, and as well as from Scotland and England, we had two from Australia over Christmas. After having had Dr and Mrs Keith Graham from Australia on the staff here for many years, it is good to continue the link with that country. These links through the medical students are fascinating. Heather, one of those with us now, is the great-great niece of Dr T.T. Thomson who was one of the early missionary doctors in Chickballapur!

Chickballapur had a flying visit from Mrs Indira Gandhi in December before the General Elections. She had an intensive tour of the State for several days, doing 20-minute flights by helicopter, with a 20-minute meeting in various towns. In spite of this, her party was defeated in Karnataka. The new Chief Minister and the Janata Party are settling in and attempting to improve conditions in the State. There is a great shortage of water and electricity. Daily there are power cuts and many of the wells have gone dry. Our well near the bungalow soon produced grey coloured water after a few buckets are drawn and the hospital tank often goes dry, as there is no electricity to pump water from the bore well.

Last Christmas was busier than ever as we had functions to arrange and attend in two hospitals this time. Immediately after, we were straight into preparations for the hospital's 70th Anniversary Celebrations. Now, comes the clearing up, but that is being left for the moment whilst this letter is written. We hope that it will reach you in time for Easter to let you know we are coming to life again like the spring flowers. Leslie was kept busy (after his outpatients' clinics, ward rounds, operations, committee meetings and fortnightly visits to Channapatna) writing a report and articles for the souvenir brochure and appeal leaflet for distribution around the town and district. The following is an extract from the appeal leaflet, which was a means of bringing in some funds.

On 26 February 1913, the Deputy Commissioner of Kolar District performed the opening ceremony of the Wardlaw Thompson Hospital, now known as the Church of South India Hospital, Chickballapur. It was a daring venture, building a 60-bedded hospital where no medical work was done previously. Most hospitals started in huts or even tents but this one began with an excellent set of buildings, which have stood the test of time very well. Seventy years is a lifetime by human standards, but the C.S.I. Hospital is not thinking of retiring but rather of expanding activities. The need for its existence is as great as ever, and its opportunities for new fields of service are limitless. It must change to suit the needs of the times.

In 1913, the hospital staff consisted of twelve people, of whom four were doctors. Today, the staff numbers 90 people of whom seven are doctors. During 1982, we have welcomed to the staff Dr Albert Kundargi and Dr Prema Kundargi. Dr Prema Kundargi is an experienced Obstetrician and Gynaecologist with much experience in major hospitals in Karnataka. Dr Albert Kundargi has trained in Eye Surgery and Ear, Nose and Throat Surgery and has also acquired the skill of anaesthetist, which is essential in a hospital with a major surgical programme. In order to give basic equipment and facilities for these doctors, the hospital has had to spend Rs. 30,000 for the urgent replacement of our X-ray machine. The old one, which had given excellent service over many years, broke down and could not be repaired. Our own funds are exhausted and we hope that the people of Chickballapur and the surrounding towns and villages who have benefitted from this hospital's work will come to its aid now and enable us to provide an even better service in the next 70 years of the life of the hospital.

What are our needs? The Board of Management has started to draw up a Master Plan to assess the future direction of the hospital's work and then to plan for the necessary buildings, staff and equipment to carry this out. Among the urgent requirements is a new building for the Pharmacy Department, which is working under difficulty in an old cramped building at present. We also require improved facilities for the doctors and for the patients' records in the Outpatient Department. Severely ill patients, who are having intensive care, are scattered at present in different wards of the hospital. If we had a small ward close to the present operating theatre, such patients could be kept there. As the number of our staff increase daily we need more staff quarters.

As well as helping to type out the material for the brochure and programmes etc., Betty was involved in visits to the printers to check on the copy, canvassing the local shopkeepers for advertisements to help pay for the brochure, sorting out articles for sale at the hospital Open Day on 26 February, making pots of yoghurt for sale, arranging for calendars to be printed etc.

Now, inspired by the many well-wishers who shared in our celebrations— messages from the Prime Minister, Chief Minister, Assistant Commissioner, donations from individuals and groups, we go forward into the future with our hands in the hands of the Master. As King George VI quoted in a Christmas message… "Put your hands into the hand of God. That will be to you better than light and safer than a known way."

21 April. As we hear from Grace that the duplicating machine, which produces this circular letter, has broken down, there is time, and space, to add some more news.

Some of you have been asking about our ambulance. It has been giving very good service, and apart from a few punctures and several tyre re-treads and two new tyres it has needed very little repair. Until last week! After its regular service (every 4,000 km), it was no sooner parked in the garage than it had to go out to collect a patient from a nearby village. About midnight Prakash our driver came

128

to report that he had been in an accident. The road was under repair and a temporary wall had been built across the road, with no warning lights, a lorry coming in the opposite direction (with no less than FOUR headlights on full beam!) came towards him, blinding him so that he could not see the wall ahead, but crashed into it nevertheless. The bumper, radiator and battery were bashed in. Fortunately, neither he nor any of the patient's relatives were injured. The passengers were flung forward and Prakash fell against the driving wheel. He came back in a lorry and a mechanic was able to get the ambulance into second gear to drive back the 12 km to Chickballapur. In the meanwhile, other arrangements had to be made to collect the patient and bring her to the hospital. There were two days holidays for the Hindu New Year—Ugadi Festival—immediately after the accident, so we had to wait six days to get the ambulance back in use. How we missed it! It really is a boon—not only for patients but also for our weekly dispensary trips, visits to Channapatna Hospital, and shopping expeditions.

Our roads are being resurfaced just now and the workers and their families live 'in-situ'—literally—in the empty tar drums, which have been cut open and flattened and made into crude shelters. I was able to get some pictures of the various processes as they built their 'tin can alley' just outside the hospital. Early one morning as we passed, a group of men, women and children were gathered around a smoky fire with a rice pot bubbling on top, listening to a radio, which was blaring forth cinema music from inside one of these homes.

On Palm Sunday, we appeared on television (only closed circuit). We were in St Mark's Cathedral, Bangalore, for the consecration of our new Bishop Rt. Rev. Dr Constantine D. Jathanna. There were several T.V. sets in the cathedral for those who sat behind pillars or outside in the marquee. It was a marvellous service, mainly in English but with various items in the three local languages.

A public reception for Bishop Jathanna was planned for Sunday 17 April at 6 pm in Bishop Cotton Girls School, Bangalore. We arrived at 4 pm and sat in the gardens reading and doing crosswords until 5:30 pm. There was no sign of the school hall being opened for the function, and eventually, we checked with the gateman who knew nothing about it! Then the headmistress appeared and said the programme had been postponed until 3 May. Talk about being too early for dinner!

We were in time, though, to attend the evening service at St Andrew's Kirk and enjoyed singing Psalm 23 to Crimond with the 100-year-old pipe organ giving the right atmosphere. A change from the little pedal organ, which has Leslie pumping like mad in his attempts to make any sound come out! We have at last tracked down an organ repairer, and he says he thinks the bellows need repairing.

Many thanks to all who have written to us during the year and to those who have sent parcels of used clothing, Christmas cards and other gifts. We appreciate them all very much, and the encouragement we have from knowing that you are interested in our work here. Thank you all, for your helping hands.

Betty and Leslie.

Letter 23
Meeting Medical Students in London.
Mrs Gandhi's Assassination. Bhopal

Chickballapur
10 December 1984

Dear Friends,

"Don't you feel the cold here?" How often we were asked this during our two months in Britain last autumn. We usually replied that we did not feel the cold, but in any case, we enjoyed the change of climate. Probably the only day we felt cold was when we tried to repair the gale damage to our garage by nailing new felt on the roof. The rain gutter on the garage, as well as the sparrows' bathwater had frozen solid overnight. As we worked, snow began to fall but did not last long. Now, here we are shivering in Chickballapur. Leslie had put his woollen pullover away in its plastic bag until the next furlough but he had to put it on to stop shivering in the daytime. His normal wear in Chickballapur is a short-sleeved shirt all year round. His jacket comes out only for the Christmas Eve carol singing, which usually lasts until 2 am and the midnight service to welcome in the New Year. We are told this abnormally cold weather is due to cyclones coming into India with relatively cold weather and prolonged rain. It seems the weather here is ever-changing—rain at all seasons—just like Bonnie Scotland!

It was good to meet so many of you when we were home. We are sorry that some of you were missed. It just was not possible to visit everybody in the time available, or along our routes, which stretched from London to as far north as Montrose. We were fortunate again to have a car during our stay, and our little red Mini travelled very well—over 2,000 miles—all over Scotland and for a wonderful week of holiday over the roads of the Island of Bute in the Firth of Clyde. We managed to explore the whole island, along the roads and footpaths, as well as over the hills and marshes. The calm water of Kilchattan Bay was very tempting. Our favourite Indian beach near Madras has warm seawater and hot sunshine, but such strong waves that swimming is impossible. Here we had calm seas but very cold air and water. We can't have everything! But we agree with our car sticker... 'Bute is Beautiful!'

One innovation, which was very successful, was a meeting in London for those who had visited Chickballapur and those who plan to come in the next two years. They were able to exchange travel tips and we were all able to see slides and photographs of the hospital at Chickballapur and the tourist spots of India. Betty now spends much of her time in correspondence with medical students and nurses who wish to come for a few months to India to widen their experience. We try to meet them in Bangalore, and then their food has to be arranged. She has been looking after them so well that they go home and tell others and we now have a constant stream of applicants and bookings up to 1988.

They see a very different type of patient and different ways of investigation and treatment from what they have known in the electronic marvels that teaching hospitals in Britain have become. Some of the medical students can do as they please during their elective period with us: others are required to do a study project while they are in India. We too have learned from the many things they discover as they probe some particular aspect of an Indian hospital. We have had research in such things as the delay in coming for treatment by leprosy patients, and attitudes to infant feeding.

We hope that their interest in the Third World and India, in particular, will remain with them, as they get involved in the business of their medical careers.

There is certainly a shortage of news from India these days to maintain interest. Being in Britain at the time of Mrs Gandhi's assassination, we probably saw more of it on T.V. than we would have had in India. The papers here are still discussing the causes and the arrests of those responsible. No doubt, trials will drag on and on, as do all court cases in India. Certainly, many others seem to have been involved, and it says little for the Security Services that such activity was not revealed to Mrs Gandhi—or perhaps she just ignored warnings. In this regard, it was interesting to read an article in a Bangalore daily paper on this subject on the day when we returned to Chickballapur.

Besides the desire for revenge, which caused attacks by Hindus on Sikhs, the writer mentioned also the activity of undesirable elements in society who take advantage of any disturbance to indulge in looting. The initial reaction by the authorities was slow on the first day, and unrest was allowed to continue unhindered and so it grew worse. No doubt, there were some other reasons such as individuals settling personal vendettas under cover of the other violence. However, this violence is now being overshadowed by the intense activity of the election to be held on Christmas Eve in most States in India. The Congress Party are using photographs of Mrs Gandhi on all their posters. 'Help us finish her work.' they say. If I remember right, that slogan did not do Winston Churchill much good in 1945. We will see what happens at the polls.

There are many headaches for the Election Officers. One of those is that, for the sake of illiterates, every voting paper had to bear the name and an approved symbol (e.g. farmer, cycle, cow etc.) for each candidate. How do you manage when there are 80 candidates in one constituency? Special ballot boxes have to be made to hold such large ballot papers. Most of the candidates are 'independents', but in most places, the official Congress or Opposition candidates have much chance of getting a majority. Like the President in the US, many of the candidates are film stars. Personalities are more important than policies. The main Congress advertisements and speeches drew terrifying pictures of the chaos and strife that will follow the election if anyone except themselves is elected. "Will your groceries list of the future include acid bulbs, iron rods, daggers?" (The Congress symbol for elections is a hand.)

However, in the last few days, all has been overshadowed by events in Bhopal. We suppose that in the UK, the daily T.V. pictures of rows of the dead in the fields of Ethiopia, which were so common when we were in Britain, have been replaced by longer rows on the grounds of the hospital in Bhopal. In arresting the head of the parent firm, the Indian authorities are placing this alongside other instances where multinational firms have one standard for the rich west and a far inferior standard for the Third World. It is easy to see the lives killed in this case but it is far more difficult to count the cases killed by inadequate safety care in many factories, or by the drugs banned in the US and then sold as 'special offer—10% off' in India by the Indian subsidiary of the American firm. Where profit takes precedence over precaution, and where a 'black' life is of less value than a 'white' one, such things will happen. Unless we have a reverence for all life, assassinations and such killings will go on forever. 'The fear of the Lord is the beginning of understanding'.

Leslie has written much of this letter in the time spent travelling to various Committees—there is a spate of them at the beginning of December. They do not start on time and the waiting time can be used profitably! There are also gaps when Committees depend on shouting matches in Kannada. Our understanding of Kannada is limited, but we can usually cope in Committees, as there is much English used—provided that there is only one speaker at a time. Unfortunately, many Committee Chairmen allow two or three persons (including himself) to shout at one another simultaneously! I doubt if even the best of our modern simultaneous translators could cope with these situations. Amazingly business is done!

On our return, we found the hospital quite busy, although the surgical wards had been half-full during our absence. One of the three young ladies who were staying in our bungalow had decorated the walls of the children's ward with flowers and animals in gay colours. It makes it look much brighter and livelier.

The students from the School of Nursing are now starting to come to the wards for their practical training, after three months in the classrooms. There are inevitably teething troubles as the students take over some of the tasks previously done by others, but we still get all the duties worked out eventually. All the students passed their first test, although two of them will need to improve if they are going to get through at the end of the year.

We are still short of a general tutor in the School, and if we do not get someone for this soon, the future of the School will be in jeopardy. The examining authorities will not allow us to continue with ten girls unless we obtain another tutor. Our salary scales are so low and tutors so scarce in India that any who are available can easily get better-paid jobs elsewhere. Without raising all the staff salaries, we cannot raise one group only. This would mean increasing our income by much more each year. For that, we would have to start some new profitable work or increase our present charges by a considerable amount. Our next Board Meeting will have to consider all this. In the meantime, we would be glad if a trained Sister Tutor from the UK would offer her services for a few months.

The nurse at present with us for four months, although not a trained tutor, and so not acceptable by the Examining Authorities, has been a great help in teaching English to the students. As well as involving them in conversation, she has been producing medical crosswords for them and having them read a Shakespeare play, which they are enjoying.

There is no possibility of solving our problems by bringing money from abroad. From 1 January 1985, everyone in India is required to obtain prior permission from New Delhi before the banks will cash a foreign cheque. It will take at least six months, says our Bishop before the system will start to work, and then we can only guess how long the delays will be. There are already enough delays in carrying out projects, so that from the time of planning and estimating to the time of completion, costs have risen so much that grants are inadequate to complete the project as planned.

We are still hoping that our School of Nursing Project will be taken up soon enough to start building in time to have some accommodation for new students next July. Several UK friends have promised to help by special efforts and the Glasgow Christian Fellowship are giving part of a Third World Flag day in Glasgow for this project, but it will take a few flag days to raise £35,000 (which is our need at today's prices) to complete the building.

As we write, Christmas greetings are arriving. We are glad to have your news. This letter will not reach you until after Christmas, but we hope that you all had a very happy Christmas and that the love and joy of the Christmas Season will last with you throughout 1985.

Betty and Leslie

Letter 24
Leprosy Ward, Visitors, Volunteers and Students

Chickballapur
20 July 1986

Dear Friends,

You must be wondering what has happened to Betty and Leslie Robinson. It is so long since you had a circular letter from us. It is not that we have forgotten you but that several attempts at writing this letter have never got beyond the first page (or first paragraph in some cases!) Some urgent problem then intervenes and the matter has to be left. When we come back to our first writing, we find it is so out-of-date that we must start again. Leslie is starting this while he sits in a special Diocesan Council meeting concerned with the Constitution of the Diocese. The meeting is due to last for three days. At the present rate of progress, the business will last for 30 days. We have difficulty in keeping enough people in the hall to maintain a quorum to pass any amendment. The result is that three Bible studies, of a very high standard by our three youngest presbyters, have been used to fill gaps in the timetable. It is divine justice for the last Council when all the Bible studies were squeezed out of the timetable for discussion of the business! So far, we have rejected most of the amendments, which suggests that the original constitution drafters did better than the present generation had given them credit for. Laws and Constitutions are necessary for the efficient running of any institution but we so easily get tied up in these matters and have no freedom to get on with the essential purpose and work for which we exist.

The work in the hospital seems to increase day by day. We have been very busy preparing for the opening of the new Leprosy Ward on 6 July by our Bishop. The final work on the ward had to be done day and night in order to have it ready for the sixth, which is our Bishop's birthday, on which he always likes to open some new building or project. He will be visiting England during August and September this year so some of you may have a chance to meet him. The ward consists of two rooms, which can take five beds each and will enable us to give more accommodation for any leprosy patients who have ulcers or various reactions or other severe diseases requiring admission. There are bathrooms and toilets attached to the wards. We have given the name of E. R. Sabapathy to this new ward. The word 'leprosy' still carries a stigma for some people and we hope someday that we will no longer have leprosy patients needing a ward. That day is still decades away but we felt we wanted to honour Sabapathy also for the selfless sacrificial way in which he cared for the village patients especially those with leprosy. He went from village to village in all seasons, heedless of his own health, seeking out the patients, bringing them for treatment and seeing that they continued to take their tablets. We all miss him much and look for someone else to continue the work he started.

Our leprosy work has received a very welcome boost from the American Leprosy Mission. One of their field staff during a tour of India came to visit his niece who was a nurse staying with us for a few months. He saw our leprosy work and obtained for us substantial grants to complete the Sabapathy Ward, to finance the treatment for the leprosy patients and to buy a motorcycle and microscope for the rural leprosy work. With new and powerful drugs becoming available, the treatment for leprosy patients is expensive but can promise at least some of them a cure within six to twelve months, and all of them can have the disease controlled. As those under treatment soon cease to be capable of infecting others, the rate of spread of the disease should be greatly reduced. However, there are still many undiagnosed cases in the community and these we need to find. We hope that with the funds made available by the American Leprosy Mission we can contribute to the search for these people in our area. The Government has an official 'search' programme, but in many cases, due to lack of staff, this is not implemented.

On 13 July, we admitted ten new nursing students to give us the third class in the School of Nursing. For the first time, we had more eligible candidates than seats and had to make a choice on the basis of the entrance exam and their scholastic record. The new School of Nursing building has only reached the ground floor window level as the person making the bricks has had difficulty in getting the materials for making them. We hope to have an adequate supply by the end of July to continue building. We had no accommodation for the new students but had to shift some of the School of Nursing lecture rooms to the new Leprosy Ward and give these rooms for the students to live in.

Dr Prema Kundargi took over as Treasurer in April this year. After preparing the past year's accounts for audit and initiating her and the other office staff into the accounting system, neither of us should be so involved in the keeping of account books in future, and this should make it easier to hand over when going on furlough.

Now we are in the midst of getting our registration papers and stamps in passports etc. to enable us to go on furlough and return to India. If all goes well, we leave Chickballapur on Friday 22 August and return on 24 October, flying this time via Delhi with KLM to Amsterdam, London and Edinburgh. We plan to attend the Congregational Union of Scotland Assembly in St Andrews from 17 to 21 September and then the C.S.I. Day in London on 27 September. We hope to see many of you there, to thank personally those who have been helping to raise funds for the School of Nursing building. We hear of various means of raising money—buying bricks, filling in cards in order to win a pen, running in the London marathon, cheese and wine party, coffee mornings, musical evening etc.

As we did in 1984 when we were on leave, we plan to have a get-together of old and new medical students, nurses and doctors who have spent/hope to spend some time with us in Chickballapur. This will be held at C.W.M. Livingstone House, 11 Carteret Street, London SW1H 9DL (opposite St James Park underground) on Friday 26 September from 11 am onwards, with lunch from about 2 pm. Anyone interested is welcome to come and as the newspapers report, 'take this as a personal invitation' and be sure to bring any photographs and slides with you. We hope to have another day in Scotland—possibly in Edinburgh— for those who are not able to come to London.

Since we were last in the UK, we have had 20 medical students, nine nurses and two doctors from the UK spend some time with us. We have been very glad of their help and all have fitted in well at home. We have also had 36 visitors! These included William Cutting, Barbara Graham from Australia, Stephen and Helen Smith with whom Betty travelled to India in 1966, Eileen Thompson from CWM, two couples from Glasgow Christian Fellowship, Smyths from Edinburgh attending a meeting of astrophysicists in Bangalore and two English cyclists on their way from Kerala to Kashmir. Sometimes, we have been rather overcrowded with twelve to be accommodated so there has been some shifting around of beds from room to room—and for one night we had a nurse on night duty sleeping in a bed during the day and another visitor sleeping in the same bed at night! If our numbers continue to increase, we may have to do more of this!

Bangalore, 35 miles away, is growing fast. A recent newspaper article states that it now has a population of 4½ million. High-rise buildings for offices, shops and houses are sprouting everywhere and the traffic becomes more congested daily with many more mopeds, scooters, motorbikes and a variety of Indian made cars in bright colours. Buses are always overcrowded and the three-wheeled auto rickshaws are now allowed to take three passengers instead of two. We have frequent visits to Bangalore for committees, shopping for hospital supplies and the occasional meal out in one of the many new restaurants. We usually return from such trips exhausted, and glad to be living in the country with fresh air, no pollution and more open spaces all around.

Two large industrial estates are marked out on the outskirts of Chickballapur and many small factories are coming up. What with other industries stretching out from Bangalore also, it will not be long until Chickballapur is a suburb of Bangalore! The road between Chickballapur and Bangalore (National Highway No. 7) is fairly straight and in good condition for most of the way, BUT a narrow-gauge railway line crosses the road five times and the main railway line twice. Before and after each of these level crossings a series of ridges, meant to slow down the traffic, have been placed across the road. One either bumps slowly over all these ridges or speeds over them in a bus with teeth rattling and bones shaking!

Another new factory has been built in the midst of villages west of Chickballapur, with Japanese collaboration to make useful yarn out of the waste from the silk spinners of this area. It is a very up-to-date factory with beautiful gardens all around it. Betty was there at the official opening of the factory when officials from Japan came and were welcomed by bedecked elephants. Leslie spent his lunch-time there one day recently to discuss with the Managing Director about our Rural Dispensary staff doing a twice-weekly clinic there. Most of the factory workers come from the surrounding villages, which are without any other medical faculties, except for those where our Rural Dispensary ambulance stops already.

Church News. On 6 July, before opening the Leprosy Ward, Bishop Jathanna unveiled the foundation stone of a new church building to be erected near our bungalow. The present church, originally built as a Memorial Hall rather than as a church, is not big enough for the present congregation and most Sundays there is an overflow onto the verandas around the building. An estimate of about Rs. 400,000 has been given for the new building and the local congregation has to raise half of this amount and then the diocese will give the remainder. So we press on with various fundraising efforts.

The Tamil Church, which Leslie attended in Bangalore when he worked there, recently enlarged its building and extended the altar. We attended a Thanksgiving Service for this and Leslie had a warm welcome from many of the members who still remembered him from over 20 years ago. A Christian Government leader (President of the State Congress Party) was invited to release the souvenir brochure giving the history of the church and reports on its various activities. He presented Leslie with the first copy.

Last month a leading Indian evangelist came to Bangalore for a day's programme. In the morning, some of us attended St Mark's Cathedral for the commissioning of a new Sister in the C.S.I. followed by a sermon given by the evangelist. Expecting crowds, the service including communion was held outside on the church grounds. By the time the service commenced, 2,000 chairs were filled and about another 2,000 were standing all around. In the evening, an open-air rally was held in a stadium with seating for 50,000 and it too was filled to capacity. Some of our visitors attended this and returned soaked through, having sat for hours in a thunderstorm with no protection! Reminds us of the visit of the Archbishop of Canterbury (Robert Runcie) to Bangalore. On a previous visit 23 years ago, he had arrived in a downpour. On the day prior to the recent public meeting when Karnataka was suffering from severe drought, he had been asked to pray for rain. Just before he arrived for the open-air gathering, there was heavy rain and last minute arrangements were made indoors instead. In the Archbishop's opening remarks he said that in future an appropriate welcome banner could say, "Runcie renowned rainmaker". Let's hope when he comes to speak at C.S.I. Day in London on 27 September, he doesn't bring rain with him then!

This is the monsoon season and we are having quite good rains this year, very much needed as many of the wells and reservoirs are dried up. The lack of rain also affects the electricity supply and the latter is now rationed. We hope the rain does not follow us to Scotland but that we may have good summer/autumn weather when we are on leave.

We hope to be able to borrow or buy a car to use during our two months' leave. We would be glad to hear from anyone with one available. The little red Morris mini we had two years ago was very useful and enabled us to get around easily.

Another item on our 'wanted' list—Church of Scotland hymnbooks (Revised edition of 1927). We use these hymnbooks daily for staff morning prayers in the hospital chapel and with our increased numbers of student nurses and visitors, we could do with more copies. These could either be sent by book post direct to us in India or passed on to us when we are in the UK.

Many thanks to all who have written to us during the past two years, sent magazines, gifts and donations and support us in so many ways. We look forward to seeing some of you soon.

Betty and Leslie

Letter 25
Portable X-Ray Machine. Reprinting
'Hot Surgery' by Dr Cecil Cutting

Dunfermline
3 October 1988

Dear Friends,

Greetings to all our friends, and apologies for the non-appearance of a newsletter for a long time. No excuse, except plenty of other jobs, which seemed more urgent—including patients who take most of Leslie's time during the hours of daylight and a lot of night too, in Chickballapur.

However, we are back in Dunfermline, or at least based in Dunfermline, from 3 September until 3 November. We have already been touring around Glasgow, St Andrews, London, Bishop's Stortford, and today we are at home before going off tomorrow for a few days holiday at Sannox. We need a day at home to get the washing done and finalise plans for this month. We have been trying to fit in as many places and people as possible, especially friends in England whom we missed on our last furlough. We shall be going to Oxford on 15 October to the wedding of Andrew Husselbee and Jane Bayley, two young people who came to Chickballapur at different times but met in England at Chickballapur reunions. Just in case there is any Oxbridge jealousy, we are going to Cambridge on 29 October for an orientation weekend organised by Action Health 2000. At present, in Chickballapur, we have a doctor and a nurse tutor—Julie and Jenny—who have been sent to us by Action Health 2000. They are very helpful and useful in the hospital and we hope for more of similar quality from Action Health 2000 in future. On our travels to and from Cambridge and Oxford, we hope to meet some of you who live in the Midlands and North of England. It will not be possible to see everybody but we will try to meet as many as possible as we go about in our little hired car.

What has been happening in Chickballapur since we last wrote? It has been a very busy period with the wards well filled. Last year there were over 900 deliveries in the hospital, keeping Dr Prema, our gynaecologist and obstetrician very busy, especially during the months when there was no junior lady doctor to help her. Now, as well as our Eye and E.N.T. Surgeon, we have added an Orthopaedic Surgeon. Dr Manjunath is a young man born in Chickballapur and trained in Bangalore University. He has a good knowledge of the theory and is fast acquiring the necessary practical experience. It is a relief to Leslie not to have to deal with the fractured bones and other accident cases.

During the past year, we received a gift of some pieces of equipment from the churches in Germany. Amongst these were a portable X-ray machine and a new operating theatre table. The X-ray machine has proved most useful to our new orthopaedic surgeon for checking the position of fractured bones in the operating theatre. In Britain, one of the most frequent jobs done by an orthopaedic surgeon is to pin a fractured hip. As the population of India ages, so more cases of this condition present to the hospital. Previously Leslie was only able to put these patients into a plaster cast, which they had to tolerate for three months; not very easy especially in the hot season. Some of them, stayed all the time in the hospital; some of them stayed a few weeks and some of them managed to cope at home until the three months were up and the plaster could be removed. Now, they can have an operation, thanks to the orthopaedic surgeon and the portable X-ray machine. Within a few days, they can be out of bed and walking with crutches—a much happier state of affairs.

The other new acquisition was an operating table. The previous table was gifted on the 25th anniversary of the hospital, and it gave good service for 50 years. The operating theatre has not changed in these 50 years, apart from some painting, and really requires to be replaced. We cannot stop the work in it for long enough to allow us to repair it. The lovely big glass window filling most of the north wall is now crumbling, thanks to the activity of the termites in its wooden frame. Thus, our plans are for a new theatre, on more modern lines, with the necessary ancillary rooms. We hope to build this in memory of Dr Cecil Cutting who served as a surgeon in Chickballapur for 30 years.

Three people who have given their life's service to Chickballapur died within a few months of each other… Sister Lisbeth Morch and Mr E.R. Sabapathy in November 1983 and Dr Cecil Cutting in February 1984.

Sister Morch served as Nursing Superintendent for 30 years. During most of that time, she worked alone, training male nursing students and at the same time being responsible for the daily maintenance and staffing of the wards and clinics. The School of Nursing, when it was reopened in 1984 was named after Sister Morch. The new building for the School is now nearing completion and we hope it will be ready for occupation by the end of 1988. It has been a slow process completing the work and we are thankful to all our friends in Britain whose gifts have made this building possible.

Mr Sabapathy spent the latter years of his life caring for the needy of the villages and Chickballapur, especially the leprosy patients, and it was fitting that the new leprosy ward opened in 1986 was named after him.

Another three people are of interest. Just before we left for Scotland, we had a little ceremony to present armchairs to three people who were retiring during September 1988 after reaching the age of 65 years. Miss Joseph had been Ward Sister in the children's ward since she came to us a few years ago after 'early' retirement in our sister hospital in Madanapalle. Mr Isaiah and Mr Sathyaraj mark the last of the male nurses who were trained in this hospital by Sister Morch. They have remained all their working lives in the same hospital. Both have given good service for many years, ever seeking to be faithful to the principles Sister Morch taught them. Brother Isaiah came from a poor family to a Christian Boarding School many years ago. Some of the missionaries connected with the school saw the need of his family and helped him to come from his village to the School of Nursing in Chickballapur where he managed to obtain his nursing qualification. He married another nurse from Jammalamadugu Hospital and was blessed with three sons. By much saving and sometimes borrowing, he managed to educate his sons and get them college training. As is the Indian custom, Isaiah also had to find wives for his sons and deal with the expenditure for their marriages, again requiring all his savings and loans as well. Now, as he retires he has little savings to help him. Neither the State nor the hospital for which he has worked will provide him with a pension. The Church of South India is just beginning to plan a scheme for pensions for all the workers in medical institutions. He gets only the Provident Fund to which he and the hospital have contributed and a gratuity from the hospital. These will not last for very long. We hope to help for a little while by giving him another light job in the hospital, looking after the hospital linen. However, he will probably have to depend on his sons who are now in good jobs—engineering and teaching but have the expense right now of bringing up their own families.

Although Leslie does not have orthopaedic cases to deal with now, there are still some accidents, which come under his care. They are chiefly of two types— snake bites and burns—cases that often have to stay in hospital for a long period as they require skin grafting for areas of skin damaged beyond repair. We recently had Sunitha, a young girl aged ten, in the ward for two months after spilling hot water over the front of her tummy and legs. She had daily dressings done till the wounds were clean and then skin grafting was done covering the raw area with partial-thickness pieces of skin taken from the intact areas of her thighs. She required two sessions of this as the damage was so extensive. She remained cheery, especially when after the operation she did not require dressings every day and could start to walk again.

We get many children with burns like this but much worse are the young brides who come to us with burns due to burning paraffin. Sometimes, this is an accident from a paraffin stove mishandled and exploding, but in recent years dowsing with paraffin and igniting it has been one of the most common forms of suicide. Occasionally it is murder, where there is a family feud over the dowry being inadequate. As modern luxuries like T.V. sets and motorcycles become available, greed for them leads some people to fall into such inhuman temptations.

Talking of temptations leads to the original Tempter and there are still plenty of snakes in India, some of which can bite with damaging effects. If the patient reaches the hospital quickly, we can give an antidote and reduce the damage, but many patients come too late. They go first to the temple or try 'cures' from quacks in the villages—all sorts of things are applied as dressings to the limb with the result that there is much damage to the skin and infection to the limb. A long period of cleaning of the wound as well as improving the condition of the patient is required before operations for the repair can be undertaken. How can we get patients to come sooner for treatment? One answer is to have people in the villages who can guide them and help them. This is what we are doing with help from the Christian Medical Association of India in two groups of villages. Under the guidance and training of our hospital staff, a woman is chosen in each village who will help the people of the village to stay healthy by having the proper vaccinations and coming for ante-natal checks etc. One of our doctors visits these areas once weekly to help the village health workers with serious cases.

Betty was involved in the beginning with the Community Health Project, acting as a driver daily going around the various villages selected, doing some of the surveys, visiting the houses, taking part in meetings with the villagers etc. In January, a second driver was appointed and Betty then became responsible for getting the hospital's 75th Anniversary brochure produced in time for the celebrations on 26 February this year. We were happy that Dr William Cutting (son of Dr Cecil Cutting—a former Medical Superintendent) and his wife Dr Margot Cutting could be there to open the medical exhibition, which was held during the week's celebrations. Then on to arranging for the reprinting of Dr Cecil Cutting's book *Hot Surgery*, the proceeds of which will go towards the new operation theatre to be built in his memory. We brought as many copies of the book as we could carry in our luggage and have been selling these as we go around.

We also have tea towels at £1.50 produced for the hospital's anniversary, and retractable ballpoint pens at 20p each, and hope that the sale of these and donations will soon help us reach our target of £20,000 for the operation theatre.

We are very grateful to Grace Dunlop for agreeing to act as our sales representative as well as illustrating, typing, duplicating and posting our circular letter.

For nearly 20 years, Anthony looked after the kitchen in our bungalow. Even in the last few years, when he had 'retired', he would come and help on special occasions or when his daughter and successor, Jayasheela, was off sick. He was in and out of the hospital in the past year and was gradually getting weaker and more breathless. One of his other daughters, Rosemary, had just completed her first profession on the way to becoming a nun and was at home for a holiday. There was a little celebration for that, and for Jayasheela's sons, two lovely little boys, Andrew aged 3 and Ajey Dev 6 months. A day or so after this Anthony felt worse and requested to be discharged from the hospital to go home. There he had a bath and sat in bed and later that day died peacefully. He was a wonderful character, always full of fun and stories of his many experiences working for many different kinds of 'masters'.

Many thanks to all who have written to us during the past two years. We are grateful for your interest and support, even if we do not reply.

Betty and Leslie

Letter 26
Hospital's Foundation 70th Anniversary

Chickballapur
27 March 1990

Dear Friends,

Our first attempt at writing a circular letter was started on 26 November 1989 when we put as the heading Greetings for Christmas and the New Year. Apart from a few paragraphs, the letter was never completed and now as today is the Telugu New Year Festival of UGADI when it has been relatively quiet in the hospital, our aim is to sit down and give you our news on this NEW YEAR'S DAY and hopefully reach you in time for Easter.

On 26 November, we celebrated the 80th anniversary of the laying of the foundation stone of the hospital by Rev. E. P. Rice, an L.M.S. missionary. The buildings were opened on 26 February 1913, and it is usually the latter anniversary which we celebrate—as we did in a grand way in 1988 for the 75th anniversary. However, we thought the 80th anniversary of the start of the building was also worthy of recognition. The present pastor of the C.S.I. Rice Memorial Church in Bangalore was our guest preacher while our local pastor led the Service of Thanksgiving. The service was held outside in front of the hospital chapel, using the steps of the chapel as the platform. The congregation sat under the cork trees—safe enough at 3 pm but a dangerous place when the birds roost in the trees at dusk. One of our staff had promised to provide the microphone and loudspeaker for the service but arrived only at 3:10 pm with the equipment by which time Leslie had rigged up a microphone to the loudspeaker for the electronic organ and that worked very well.

On 30 November, we celebrated the capping ceremony of this year's student nurses who joined the course in July and who had successfully completed the preliminary course. The Graduation Service for the second batch of nurses was also held that day. As well as receiving their Certificates, they had pinned to their uniform saris the Sister Morch School of Nursing badge with its emblem of Christ washing His disciples' feet and the motto 'Servants of the Servant Master'. One of the calendars with Bible texts that we had on sale over Christmas had this illustration so we had good custom from our students and staff. As usual, we sold Christmas cards (remade from old cards of previous years) and calendars—with the profit going towards the new Operation Theatre Fund. One of our UK medical students sketched three designs, which we made into blocks and printed on Christmas cards and as notelets.

Other visitors who were enthusiastic knitters revived Betty's interest in knitting and orders continue to pour in for a variety of knitwear for babies, children and adults. Proceeds from the knitting are also going to the O.T. fund, as you might guess. The knitting and crocheting circle grew with nurses interested in learning, and Jayasheela (our cook) and various members of her family—including her husband—crocheting in their spare time to help with orders. Quite a business developed with workers being paid in relation to the amount of wool used, and an almost equal amount going into the O.T. fund. Betty's 'boutique' keeps developing with orders for baby blankets and wraps for new-born babies in the maternity ward. When colourful Bombay Dyeing flannelette material was used, the request came for not only baby cot size but also single bed size sheets of the same material. Then from that to double bed size! With almost daily trips to Bangalore for these sheets and wool for the knitters, this gave Betty the opportunity to knit on the bus. Sometimes, she had the assistance of the passenger in the seat beside her to wind wool—or to 'rescue a ball of wool that blew out of the window, with passengers winding it in! Now that the summer season is upon us with a vengeance the request is for cotton saris, and this new 'business' has got off to a good start with today's Ugadi festival when the Hindus have new clothes. The Christians will be buying theirs for Easter. So yet more trips to Bangalore for the goods.

We were glad to welcome back Dr Heather (third visit) and her surgeon husband Richard Scott for almost six months. During the latter part of their stay, Leslie was forced to stay in bed for two weeks in order to let varicose ulcers in his right ankle get a chance to heal. Betty was kept busy as a 'messenger' bringing papers back and forth from the hospital. The ulcers healed eventually although Leslie spent several weeks in the clinic seeing patients with his leg stretched out on a stool. On 10 April, we had the ground-breaking ceremony for the new Operation Theatre block being built in memory of Dr Cecil Cutting. We hope that it will be ready for use by 10 April next year, or soon after. Last week air-conditioners were fitted in the two major theatres and today work began in fitting oxygen pipes. With at least one, if not two, emergency Caesarean operations daily last week (which meant postponing other major surgery) we look forward to the opening of this much needed new building.

We had a brief visit last month from Bishop Kenneth Gill, former Bishop in this diocese and now in Newcastle. He took part in the ground-breaking ceremony for a new community hall cum library for the School of Nursing. A group in Germany in a programme called Women to Women Project has donated the cost of this building so no fundraising is necessary on our part.

What we DO need to raise funds for is a new ambulance to replace our wedding present Mahindra diesel jeep ambulance, which regretfully we had to sell at the end of January. It was in need of major repair and as it was nearly ten years old, we were advised to buy a new one instead. We got a good price for it but must add to that sum in order to buy a similar new vehicle. At present, we have the use of an old English Bedford van belonging to another diocesan institution but it too requires a rebore soon as it belches out black smoke from the exhaust. One of the hospital staff made a cardboard model of an ambulance, and this is on display in the maternity ward where patients come for antenatal checks. Slowly the coins drop in. As we seek further help from friends, we are bold to invite all who receive this circular letter to send a donation towards a new ambulance. We are very grateful for the many that have helped, both individually and through churches and other groups, with our School of Nursing building (completed and full to overflowing) and Operation Theatre building.

We wrote our last circular letter in Dunfermline in October 1998 when we were on furlough and staying with Betty's parents. We had a telegram with the sad news of the death of Betty's father on 4 November 1989. Her mother has now gone to stay with her younger daughter in Cowdenbeath and has sold her home in Dunfermline. Our base while on furlough this year (September/October) will be with Betty's sister Mrs May Scott, whose two daughters are married and now have two children each.

Indians often ask if the various medical students and other volunteers who stay with us are our children! We are glad to have all these helpers, many of whom keep in touch and continue to support our work, and some return after qualifying or further training. We are in need of an anaesthetist for our new theatre block so such a person would be gladly welcomed. These visiting students also get involved in other activities outside the hospital, sometimes through contacts they have made before coming to Chickballapur, sometimes through specific interests they have, like music. Several who have been gifted musically have been thrilled with a local music teacher who introduced them to Carnatic music—the Indian music that has its own scales and forms different from western music.

We too are in the news—or rather, in print. Two English cyclists who spent a night with us some years ago have written a book about their cycling trip from Kashmir to Kanyakumari called *Ram Ram India* (by Alex. Thomson and Nick Rossiter. Collins). Well written and very descriptive.

We end this belated annual circular with Easter greetings and look forward to meeting some of you when in the UK in the autumn.

Betty and Leslie

Letter 27
Furlough September/October. Nurses' Graduation. More Building Plans

Chickballapur

18 November 1990

Dear Friends,

Starting again in November, in the hope, this will reach you by Christmas. It is now ten days since we arrived back from furlough, and we have been busy since our return. We had a pleasant although sleepless journey from Edinburgh via London and Brussels and arrived at 3 am in Bombay. We waited a long time for the bus from the one airport to the next and eventually arrived at the check-in desk at 6:15 am to be informed that the flight was 6:40 am but was closed—and the officials would not let us through. No speedy Edinburgh shuttle here! Then the not-so-simple matter of changing the booking to the next flight! After an hour of visiting several officials and desks and demands for a new ticket to be paid in sterling, we eventually agreed to pay in rupees 25% of the price plus the increase in the fare since we had bought the ticket originally. That got us to Nos. 59/60 on the waiting list for a flight at 4 pm. We spent the day on hard plastic chairs at Bombay airport, and at about 3:30 pm, we heard our names called so we could get on the flight. Then we learned it was delayed until 5 pm—because of a bomb hoax, as we discovered later. Our new ambulance was waiting for us at Bangalore airport, and we eventually reached Chickballapur around 9 pm, weary of our travels but glad to be back and to meet the German student and his fiancé who were staying in our bungalow. They have now left on their travels around India.

We were ready for a sleep. The hospital staff planned to welcome us at the morning chapel at 7:30 am but on being awakened at 7 am we said we would NOT be up by that time and Leslie would come only later to do the Leprosy

Clinic but nothing else that morning. As soon as Leslie entered the hospital gate, the staff were summoned to the chapel and so Betty had to be called too. We were welcomed in the usual manner with garlands. It was just as well Leslie did not plan anything else for that day, as there were 153 leprosy patients (usually 100) due to his absence for two months and the fact that the previous Thursday had been a public holiday without any clinics.

The hospital had been busy during our absence with the gynaecologist (22 Caesarean operations in September) and the orthopaedic surgeon keeping busy. The political troubles and especially the Hindu-Muslim fighting had led to the imposition of restrictions and night curfew in this area so that many patients could not come to the hospital. Things are a bit more settled at present but the problems, which caused the trouble, are still not solved and our new Prime Minister will be much stretched to find a peaceful solution. The Gulf crisis with a shortage of petrol and diesel also brings its problems (fewer buses and fewer trips by our hospital vehicle) and to add to the troubles the Telegraph and Telephone staff are on strike—so communication is difficult.

There is also a shortage of kerosene and cooking gas cylinders, and frequent electric power cuts. (Instead of reheating food if a meal is delayed, we have been keeping it in stainless steel dishes in a large polystyrene box—originally used as an icebox but now as a 'hot box'.) Takes us back to our early days in India when cooking was done on firewood in a kitchen separate from the house, and then the cooked meal was placed on racks in a metal-lined wooden cupboard with a burning charcoal pot inside to keep the food warm.

In our last letter, we had asked your help in raising funds for our new ambulance, and as mentioned above this is now in use. There was a very generous response enabling us to send a cheque for £5,000 through the appropriate channels to purchase the vehicle in Bombay, and it arrived in Chickballapur at the end of September and is now in full use IF we can get the fuel for it. We are still discussing the taxation of the vehicle with the local officials who first asked for Rs. 5,000 per month! So far we have paid Rs. 800 and have been provided tax exemption completely if we sign an agreement never to make any charges for the vehicle! With two full-length stretchers and a seat for the attendant doctor or nurse, separated by a glass screen from the doctor and driver in front, and standing room height—the vehicle is indeed VERY BIG as our cook commented when she first saw it. Quite a change from our little wedding present jeep ambulance. It served us very well for nine years, covering dried up/or swollen rivers, rough country tracks—some metalled and some mere ploughed fields—as well as making many regular trips on main national highways to Bangalore and Channapatna etc. It also covered long distances with patients or dead bodies as far away as Mangalore and to the northern tips of Karnataka and Andhra Pradesh. We hope that this new 'minibus' ambulance will serve us as well.

Recently a new non-veg restaurant opened on the outskirts of Chickballapur so today we ventured out there by cycle to have Sunday lunch. The chicken biryani and curds (yoghurt) for the two of us cost Rs. 22 (about 30 pence each!) It was quite tasty but not exactly Bangalore five-star hotel standard. The restaurant looks out onto fields and Nandi Hills, with nice colourful bushes on the grounds. Our cook Jayasheela's chicken biryani the previous Sunday was much tastier! She would do well to open a restaurant! Meanwhile Betty's 'sales business' has restarted with Christmas cards, pens and calendars. We brought back some cards in our hand luggage and Betty finished trimming them to size. Jayasheela and her husband stick them onto the card (huge supply bought and printed last year and folded by hospital staff, so ready for sticking). The 'stickers' are paid 10 paise per card to encourage them and give them an extra income for Christmas expenses! Cards are on sale in the injection room in the hospital for staff and patients and business has been brisk already. Vishranthi Nilayam in Bangalore is our city outlet, and they are given 10% of the sales for their funds. The first edition of a monthly diocesan newsletter is due out on 1 December and as well as an article about the hospital written by Leslie, a note regarding sales at Vishranthi has been added! After selecting about 40 different designs for calendars, and giving the hospital's name and address for printing, the 1,000 calendars were ready within six days. Some service is prompt and speedy!

Ten student nurses will be formally 'capped' after passing their preliminary training period. Nineteen nurses who have completed their general nursing and midwifery training will graduate and be given their badges, and a stripe added to their caps. These students studied under the old scheme of three years' general nursing and seven months of midwifery. The first batch under the present scheme of three years, which includes midwifery and more community health, also graduate now. The function is taking place in the new community hall after its official opening at the end of November. From July 1991, we are expected to take 20 students per year instead of the present ten. This means we require more tutors for classroom teaching, senior staff for the wards and more classrooms and dormitory accommodation!

We are involved in making new building plans. We have submitted plans to TEAR FUND in England and hope that they will be able to help us with funding for a new building, which would have classrooms, a demonstration room, tutors' rooms and offices. The present building, which has bedrooms upstairs, and classrooms and offices downstairs would become the hostel for all students and staff nurses.

The new community hall was a gift from a Group in Germany through a 'Woman to Woman' programme of Kindernothilfe. The hall will be multipurpose—being used as a library cum study hall for the student nurses to supplement the cramped classrooms—and as a meeting place for School of Nursing and hospital functions. It has a stage and room with an attached bathroom behind it, which can be used as a guest room or changing room for dramas etc. We were happy that Bishop Ken Gill, former Bishop of this Diocese and two medical students from Germany were able to take part in the ground-breaking ceremony in February this year.

The contractor for this building was the one responsible for the Dr Cecil Cutting Memorial Operation Theatre block. This building has been well used since it was opened on 27 May this year. Slowly, as funds come in, we are able to purchase the extra equipment required for the three operation theatres. During our two months of furlough in the UK (September/October) many friends and well-wishers helped us raise some of the money required and we look forward now to ordering some of the equipment.

For the past two months and also daily since our return, there has been heavy rain and all four bedrooms in our bungalow have damp patches on the flat roof or top of the walls. We are waiting for an engineer to come from Bangalore to advise on what to do, as it may mean complete replastering of the flat roof and walls. Two bedrooms, including ours, could do with distempering, but this must wait until the reason for the dampness is found and rectified. All this we want to be cleared up before the house fills up with medical students as we need to have at least one empty room to keep the furniture of the room being repaired/painted.

We may complain of dampness while some have no home at all. A family of leprosy patients live in a pile of stones forming three walls and covered with a sheet of plastic, against a building opposite our church. Meanwhile, in front of our compound gate, a small monkey temple has been built. It has cemented stone slabs on the walls and roof, an iron grill and electric light! (George Orwell in ANIMAL FARM said, "All animals are equal, but some animals are more equal than others".) Certainly, here in India, the monkey is worshipped and revered, and this temple, like so many others, which spring up on the death of a monkey, has more facilities than many a man has. One night last week, we heard music blaring forth until 11 pm—then it started up again at 5:30 am with a lot of talking going on throughout. Strings of coloured lights decorated the shamiana (awning) erected in front of the temple. This may have been the official inauguration of the temple by a priest. We did not go out to investigate as we had plenty of 'homework' to do.

The Senior Accounts Officer in the hospital left suddenly at the beginning of August and the Treasurer had to manage with two new members of staff who joined only in July. Betty has been asked to check their work during these months and to supervise the Administration Dept. The audit for 1989–90 begun in September is still unfinished so there are many loose ends to be tied up and ledger adjustments between accounts to be finalised. It is very difficult to find capable staff as even those with B.Com. degrees don't understand how to keep accounts. Handwriting and figures leave a lot to be desired too, with rubbing out and overwriting and seemingly no pride in doing neat work. Dr Keith Graham's account books are excellent examples of how books should be kept.

After having to apply annually to the police for 'extension of stay in India', we are happy to have received from the Government of India Ministry of Home Affairs in New Delhi permission for a period of five years until 1 May 1994. (We had applied for this in April 1989—and only JUST now received the information. This new rule applies to those who have been in the country for more than 20 years and we both qualified.)

We have also made a start in drawing up plans for a new outpatient department as the present one is very overcrowded. All the benches in the waiting hall are usually full and the room congested. Junior doctors have to share clinics—some rooms divided up with a part-wall only, and patients have to go here and there within the hospital for injections, laboratory tests, X-ray etc. The planned 'circular/hexagonal type' building will cater for all these departments and be adjacent to the main hospital building.

As we look back on all the additions during the past year, we look forward to yet more in the coming year.

When we left Chickballapur in September one of our nurses travelled with us to Belgium and then we saw her on a flight to Dusseldorf. A German family had supported Kaliammal during her primary and high school education and her nursing training here in Chickballapur, through Kindernothilfe. The family in Germany had kept in touch with her through letters and photos over the years but had never met. A member of the family contacted a T.V. programme (similar to *Jim'll Fix It* on UK television) and the show arranged for Kaliammal to fly to Cologne and meet her German 'family' during a programme—keeping it as a surprise for the 'foster parents' until Kaliammal appeared on the stage in front of them.

By all accounts, it was a great success for everyone concerned—and a boost for support for Kindernothilfe. Kaliammal has returned to India but not yet reported back to the hospital for duty. We look forward to hearing her impressions and seeing the video of the T.V. programme.

Before we have to burn the midnight oil—or candles when the power fails— let us end this update on the past year and close with all good wishes for Christmas and the coming year, with thanks to all who have kept in touch with us during the past year. Many thanks again to all who sent donations for our various projects and magazines, old Christmas cards, knitting patterns etc.

Betty and Leslie

Letter 28
New Community Hall. School of
Nursing. Tear Fund Support for Jeep

Chickballapur
6 March 1992

Dear Friends,

As we missed sending a Christmas circular letter, we hope this will reach you in time for EASTER at least. (Our last circular was sent on 18 November 1990—in case some think they have been missed out!) As we prepare to celebrate the Telugu New Year on 4 April, we send you all greetings for THAT New Year! In India there are many festive holidays and excuses for celebrations. We in the hospital have had a fair share of them this past year.

At the end of November 1990, our new Community Hall was opened by a German lady, daughter of Bishop Lipp, one of the founders of Kindernothilfe through which organisation a donation was received for the construction of this building. The hall is well used, not only by the student nurses and for hospital gatherings, but for wider community gatherings also. On 30 January this year, Gandhi's birthday and Leprosy Day, we gathered together all the leprosy patients who had come for the weekly outpatient clinic and showed them films on leprosy and then gave them lunch donated by a local judge before they saw Leslie for check-up and medicines. On 29 February, we had a group of 40 village women come for a day's programme on THE GIRL CHILD organised by a Hindu Social Worker in the area.

The hall has also been used for hospital social occasions and for money-raising efforts through sales and auctions—the most recent being on 26 February when we celebrated the hospital's 79th birthday. During the day, eatables and handicrafts were on sale with an auction of cast-off clothes from visiting students, and an assortment of much-prized foreign goods donated by recent visitors. In the evening in the open quadrangle of the School of Nursing, a large gathering (too many for the hall) enjoyed a Benefit Show put on by the student nurses and hospital staff. There were dance items, singing and a drama. THE FAKE DOCTOR (or 'quack' as we usually call the unqualified or semi-qualified species) not only brought out the dramatic skills of our staff but also pointed out some of the dangers of these 'get rich quick' fakes. Many of our patients' relatives were in the audience so we hope they took note of the dangers so common in the villages. The day's events brought in nearly Rs. 7,000 which was very encouraging. This money goes towards a new Outpatient Department block, which we hope to start building as soon as we receive the grant of £15,000 promised by C.W.M.

In the meantime, work has started on the new School of Nursing classroom block, with 75% of the cost donated by TEAR FUND. The ground-breaking ceremony for this building was led by Bishop Jathanna who dug the first sod, followed by several others who made a few dents with a pickaxe in the hard earth. The digging of the foundation began in earnest on 4 March and we hope to celebrate the opening by the hospital's 80th birthday next year! In July 1991, 15 students were admitted for the 3-year training. This year we are expected to take 20 students, so need bigger classrooms and more bedrooms. Once the new building is complete, the present School of Nursing block will become the Hostel for students and new staff serving their bond period of two years after training.

We are also grateful to TEAR FUND for their gift, which enabled us to buy a vehicle for the School of Nursing. This is a much-advertised TEMPO TRAX jeep, which gives good mileage. Officially meant to hold six plus driver, last week it held, quite comfortably, 7 adults and 3 children plus driver! It is painted green and white and before taking it for registration, we had painted in red on the side, SCHOOL OF NURSING, C.S.I. Hospital, Chickballapur and a large red cross front and back. This vehicle is being used to take the student nurses to nearby villages for their daily community health visits as well as for the use of patients coming to and from the hospital when the 'big' ambulance is out on the rural dispensary trips. Just yesterday, Betty drove a patient recovering from a broken hip to his village 34 km away. Meanwhile, the big ambulance, which was waiting for us when we returned from furlough in November 1990, is well used for the thrice-weekly roadside clinics, shopping in Bangalore and taking larger groups of students for educational visits to other institutions, or sightseeing/picnic excursions to the top of Nandi Hill and elsewhere. It can also take two stretchers for patients who have to lie down, or for taking dead bodies home to their villages.

We 'celebrated' the death of two colleagues last year. Sad though it was to hear of the deaths of Mrs Eleanor Cutting who served here in Chickballapur with her husband Dr Cecil Cutting for 30 years, and Dr Betty Milledge, formerly a missionary with her husband Dr Jim in Vellore, yet we and many other friends and colleagues as well as family, had Thanksgiving Services for their lives and work and witness.

Here in the hospital when patients continue to overflow the wards they are given makeshift beds on the verandas! We now officially have 175 beds but on a few occasions, the number of in-patients has been recorded as 200+! Heavy rains last year caused much damage to wards—not only requiring a new weatherproof surface on some roofs—male surgical ward, chapel, x-ray room and pump house—but also a completely new roof for the busy maternity ward. When a metre square piece of plaster fell onto a sleeping mother one night (fortunately causing only a slight graze to the blanket-covered body) the ward was evacuated and mothers and babies transferred to the recently painted leprosy wards. (The six leprosy patients were moved out to a ward veranda.) On inspection, the maternity ward roof showed cracks in the beams and necessitated the complete removal of the roof and a new reinforced concrete roof to be erected. Support scaffolding is being removed this week, and then plastering, new electric wiring and painting still to be done. March is usually a busy month for the labour ward! We have been having over 100 deliveries per month during the past year, with many complicated births—169 requiring caesarean operation during 1991. This week Dr Prema our senior obstetrician/gynaecologist conducted three caesareans in one day.

Since our new operation theatre was opened in May 1990, 1,670 major and 2,390 minor operations have been carried out. Doctors appreciate the much-improved facilities—air-conditioned changing rooms and piped oxygen etc.

In October last year, we had a sudden spate of patients suffering from snakebite and there is a nationwide shortage of anti-snake venom. Those who received the injection made quick recoveries but when our stock was depleted, and none available locally or in Bangalore, letters were sent far and wide and fortunately we were able to get a few vials. So often, there is a short supply of drugs from national drug companies and just last month an urgent telegram and phone call came asking us to return a batch of Aspirin tablets supplied recently.

We await the report as to why, and hope that the 2,000 tablets already issued to patients are not contaminated/adulterated or in any way dangerous.

Medical representatives come almost daily to visit the doctors and pharmacy, showing their latest products and seeking orders. A few bring free samples of the drug, while others have gifts of calendars, diaries, key rings, pens etc. Some of the more exotic gifts we auction in aid of the hospital funds! A recent American visitor (G.P.) brought several gifts he had received in his clinic from medical reps. Visiting medical students/nurses/doctors often bring such handouts, which help boost our sales, as everyone here likes anything foreign—although advertisement hoardings in the city say, BE INDIAN! BUY INDIAN!

During the year, we have had our usual flow of medical/nurse students, qualified nurses and doctors, as well as visits from friends on holiday in India. We have had volunteers with ages ranging from 17 to 61—and any interested in offering his/her services for a period of time—3/6/12 months—might like to contact us directly or for those in Scotland there is the Scottish Churches World Exchange Programme, 121 George Street, Edinburgh EHG2 4YN. The hospital is not officially able to employ such volunteers who come on a tourist visa but pay us for board and lodging in our house. Students who come for their elective periods pay about £1 per day for board and lodging with us.

We are grateful to all who keep in touch with us through circular letters, letters, Christmas cards etc. and for those who send gifts in response to our appeals. We are very grateful for all the support we receive and apologise for the delay in replying sometimes. This delayed annual circular is one way of keeping in touch and letting you know a little about what we have been doing. As the mango trees come into blossom and fruit begins to form, colourful jacaranda and other flowering trees brighten up the dry, dusty ground as the temperature rises, and no clouds are seen in the bright blue skies, we think of those in the UK with crocuses and daffodils coming out to celebrate Spring.

Betty and Leslie

Letter 29
Furlough September/October. New Outpatients Department

Chickballapur

22 November 1992

Dear Friends,

This comes with Christmas greetings to our many friends in the UK and other parts of the world. We have just returned from taking an English service in our local C.S.I. Church. The morning service is in the local language KANNADA. In August, our present Pastor started having an evening service in English on the second and fourth Sundays of the month, which is much appreciated by many of our student nurses and other staff whose mother tongue is not Kannada. With the pastor on leave this week, Leslie was asked to give the sermon and as he also plays the organ, he asked me to lead the service. Leslie used the poem by G.K. Chesterton, THE DONKEY, as part of his talk on the verses in Exodus 23 verse 5. Walking home in the starry night, we began thinking of the Christmas carol sung by Nina and Frederick—LITTLE DONKEY. Many village children studying in hostels celebrate what they call 'Little Christmas' on 25 November, as they will have gone to their own homes for 25 December. We celebrate Christmas at least twice in Chickballapur, with many invitations to carol services and dramas and feasts.

In the hospital, we are going to have a Christmas Sale on 25 November, with calendars and Christmas cards (recycled old cards) and tags produced by our present volunteers. Cindy (midwife) and Lesley (dentist) travelled with us on 2 November and Nicola (medical student) arrived the next day. Julia, a German pre-medical student is staying with an Indian family in Chickballapur as part of an International Cultural Youth Exchange programme. Another German medical student arrives later this week. He too can help in the busy Christmas production line! All this is geared to raise funds for the new buildings, as part of our hospital's 80th-anniversary celebrations, which will be held on 26–28 February 1993.

We were on our biennial furlough in the UK from 27 August to 2 November, but once again, we were not able to visit or even contact all whom we would have liked to see. Our base was with Betty's sister, May, in Cowdenbeath, where we were part of her enlarged family—mother, husband, daughter, son-in-law, granddaughter, grandson and new baby grandson born on 7 October. We had a caravan in the garden where we slept, and where we could accumulate parcels of woollens, old Christmas cards etc. to bring back to India, and a place to sort out slides and photos for showing as we went around. We enjoyed having 3-year-old Jody entertain us with her playgroup songs and nursery rhymes and games. It was good to be there to see the new day-old baby brother Scott and share in bath times and walks in the nearby park.

We were glad to make contact with the Scottish Churches World Exchange in Edinburgh and to meet their recruits Cindy and Lesley who are to be with us for a year.

We had been led to believe that our flight from London to Madras was non-stop but on arrival at Heathrow discovered it had a fuel stop in Dubai. We got out there and stretched our legs in the air-conditioned terminal but could see the dry dusty desert land stretching far into the distance. In Madras, we discovered that the flight time to Bangalore had been changed and then delayed, so only after a seven-hour wait did we eventually take off for the 40-minute flight to Bangalore. Our ambulance was waiting to take us the 35 miles to Chickballapur and 'home'.

After catching up on jet lag, we had a tour of the hospital to see the building works and meet many of the staff. Dr Prema, our gynaecologist, was especially glad to see us back as she and her husband had been busy with deliveries in October. Our recently opened baby nursery is full to overflowing with 11 babies needing special care—including three sets of twins this month. One set of twins, both girls, born at home, came with their mother who needed hospital attention (retained placenta 24 hours after delivery!) After a few days, one baby died, and against the doctor's orders, the mother discharged herself. Binny, the nurse in charge of the ward, found the mother and a relation walking out of the ward without the other twin baby! They did not want the remaining baby girl. Many families still treat girls as second-class citizens, and just this week, in the daily newspaper, there was an article about government hospitals in the Madras area arranging for a baby cot to be left outside the hospital door for unwanted/abandoned babies—to reduce female infanticide.

Recent shopping trips to Bangalore have meant purchases of more baby cradles for the nursery. Our bundles of new baby woollens were eagerly awaited and now various designs of baby dresses are being produced by our visitors—including one 'fashion'—two handkerchiefs tied with a bow on each shoulder to wear under the woollen top!

The two cyclones on the coast have brought heavy rains here and a drop in the temperature. Not only babies but adults too are crying out for woollens. We are grateful to all those who gave us hand knitted bonnets and jumpers for babies and children to bring back with us. Going round the various charity shops in the UK, we found many bargains of nearly new woollens, which were very tempting, but 20 kg. air luggage limited what we could bring.

Until now, there has been no dental department in the hospital, although Leslie has done some teeth pulling and simple dental treatment in the past. With the offer of dental equipment from Germany and the services of Lesley Porteous, dentist, for one year, we decided to go ahead and set one up. The German equipment has not yet arrived but within a few days of our return, we have fitted out the former Operation Theatre as a dental clinic, using an examination table and gathering together various other bits and pieces of furniture. With the electrician still fitting an overhead light and the carpenter repairing a wall cupboard door, the first patient arrived and sitting on an ordinary chair, had a tooth removed. Since then, there has been a steady queue of patients for a variety of treatments that can be done with our limited equipment so far. A visit to an American Mission Hospital in Bangalore showed us the other extreme—reclining padded chairs, fitted cupboards full of stainless steel equipment and gold pellets for crowning! We plan to have a properly fitted dental department in our new Outpatient Department building.

The site of the new O.P.D. now has several huge craters for the erection of steel pillars. The steel framework for the pillars is being assembled at the side of the site and tomorrow the architect and engineer from Bangalore are to come and check the markings of this circular-shaped building.

Piles of poles are now ready for the construction of the roof of the new School of Nursing classroom block. The central staircase up to the roof is now being constructed and we hope the cyclonic storms are over before the concrete goes on the roof.

Sixteen nurses who have completed their three-year training will be taking part in the Graduation Service on 30 November. Their white caps will have a black band added and each will be presented with a certificate and a badge. After two years' service in the hospital here as a qualified staff nurse, we hope that a few at least will continue here and one or two will be willing to go for Tutor training. We are still in need of Tutors and seeking volunteers from the UK as we are finding it difficult to get staff locally.

When we were on furlough attending the Church of South India Day gathering in Birmingham, we heard of the sudden death of the Moderator of the C.S.I. while in Germany on a visit in September. Bishop Dandin of Karnataka Northern Diocese was installed as Moderator in Madras on 12 November and seven of us from the hospital attended a welcome meeting for the new Moderator in Bangalore last week.

A new Chief Minister for Karnataka has also taken office this past week, and he has promised to clean things up. Already he has produced a Code of Conduct whereby Ministers and other government officials are to attend to their duties and be in their office during official working hours!

Thinking about the expression 'donkey work', brings us back to the beginning of this letter and the donkey illustrations. Many people complain of being given the hard 'donkey work' to do that no one else is willing to do—but the donkey in Nina and Frederick's Christmas carol had a very special job—carrying Mary to Bethlehem.

Soon we will be following the stars shining on the rooftops of the Christian houses in this largely Hindu community, as we go round singing carols on the 24th night. Many village homes will have the birth of a baby alongside the cattle and hens that share their simple thatched house.

As we celebrate Christmas this year, let us share what we have, including our talents (gifts) with others.

Betty and Leslie

Letter 30
Christmas Day Babies. Leslie 25 Years in Chickballapur Celebration

Chickballapur
28 December 1993

Dear Friends,

Writing this Christmas circular letter surrounded by strings of Christmas cards received from far and near. There are coloured strips of crepe paper streamers gathered into a central point high up in the 30 ft. high ceiling of the living room of our bungalow, with a star in the centre and another star outside on the veranda. A small artificial Christmas tree sits on the window sill. The wards in the hospital are all similarly decorated, with strings of fairy lights around a manger scene. A bed of soil with green shoots sprouting out the words, MERRY CHRISTMAS AND A HAPPY NEW YEAR sits in front of the manger.

This year about 60 student nurses and staff went round the wards on Christmas Eve singing carols, then round the staff houses in the hospital compound where we were given sweet and savoury snacks. To bed by 2 am then up in time for the church service on Christmas Day at 8 am. With the new church building still not completed, our present church was filled to overflowing with many sitting outside under the colourful shamianas (marquees) erected on either side.

After the church service, we went around the wards giving out leaflets with the Christmas story, bags of sweets to all, gifts for the children in the children's ward and woollen sweaters to the babies in the maternity ward and tubectomy ward. Our maternity ward continues to be a busy place with over 1,000 deliveries during the year. Our Christmas baby came as a second son to a woman who already had a three-year-old boy. He was given a special layette. It was sad to

166

visit one of the private wards to find a young 22-year-old mother who had a still-born baby on Christmas Day. Many patients unfortunately come to us without proper care before delivery and when it is too late for us to save the baby.

The day after Christmas, Dr Prema had to do two caesarean sections in the middle of the day. Both babies did well, but the second mother was fortunate she had come from a distant village and was very anaemic and the baby had been trying to come hand first for some hours before she reached the hospital. Many of those who have deliveries here, stay on for a tubectomy operation a few days after delivery, and others come from their village for operation 10-20 days after delivery in the village. More are accepting a two-child family but there are still those who go on forever, like the Muslim lady who delivered her tenth baby (her sixth son) on Christmas Eve. She is not interested in tubectomy!

Our family in the bungalow continues to grow with up to eleven visitors—medical students, qualified doctors, nurses and others! At the beginning of December, four of them could be seen up ladders in the children's ward decorating the walls with colourful scenes, much to the amusement and entertainment of the parents of the children.

Sadly, many of the children were too sick to enjoy the drawings. The end of 1993 has brought with it a large number of children suffering from encephalitis (brain fever). Shortly after Betty came to Chickballapur (1979), we had the first attack of this virus in our area and over 80 patients were admitted to our wards—all children, mostly between 3 and 8 years old. Every year we get a few cases in October and November, but again this year we have had a large number of them. About one-third die within a day or two, another third make a rapid recovery within ten days to resume a fairly normal life but the unfortunate ones are the others who remain in various levels of consciousness. Some can take feeds by mouth but most have to be tube-fed. Some lie quietly without any response to those around them. Some are severely spastic and limbs are continuously twisting. Some are silent and some cry for long periods. The parents watch anxiously over them during their long stay in the hospital. Some of them are able to go home eventually if the parents have learned to cope with feeding, washing, and everything else that has to be done for their child. Quite a camaraderie develops between these parents as they live together in the ward and share their similar problems.

Not only does our 'family' in the bungalow grow, but we now have 53 'daughters' in the School of Nursing. In July 1993, 20 students joined the 3-year

General Nursing and Midwifery Course, and on 30 November, they received their caps after successfully completing their preliminary training period. Fifteen nurses received black stripes on their caps and were given badges and certificates, having reached the end of their training in our School of Nursing. At this special graduation and lamp lighting service, another item was included this year—the honouring of Dr Leslie Robinson for having served in this hospital for 25 years! Much to his embarrassment, Leslie was present with a HUGE garland that had about 200 red roses strung together and that reached down to his ankles. He presented the garland to the students who took it apart and had roses in their hair the next day!

After the service, food was served on the roof of the new School of Nursing classroom block, which has been in full use since 1 July 1993. This large flat-topped roof had a marquee fitted over it and long trestle tables were laid out in rows to feed about 400 students and their families who came to attend the function and all our hospital staff and their families.

Work continues on the new Outpatient Department building, with metal doorframes arriving today. We hope that the official opening of this much-needed department can take place on the hospital's next birthday on 26 February 1994. In the meantime, two families of coolies who are working on the construction are camping out in two of the rooms. The small children play in the sand while bigger brothers and sisters carry tiles to lay on the floor, and mothers cook the family meals on small kerosene stoves out in the open air. These families have come from Tamil Nadu (our neighbouring State) to work here, and like that Family who found no room in the inn, are making do with what is available.

Many of the families who survived the earthquake recently are still homeless and continue to camp out in makeshift shelters. Many of our friends and relatives wrote to us at the time of the earthquake, having looked up maps to see how near we were to the target area. Most of us in Chickballapur slept through the slight tremors felt here though some woke up with the feeling of something pushing their beds, slight swaying movement, cassettes falling off a shelf etc. Newspapers, radio and television were full of pictures and descriptions of the sudden devastation. The exact number of those who perished will never be known. As we repair compound walls and houses built with mud mortar and brick, damaged by heavy monsoon rains these past few months, we can imagine the plight of those in houses with stone slabs on top for roofing, which collapsed on sleeping families at around 4 am. The response to appeals for help was tremendous. Our hospital staff met and decided to give one day's salary to the Diocesan Earthquake Appeal Fund.

Since Bishop Jathanna retired in July 1993, Karnataka Central Diocese has been without a Bishop. Rev. Dr K.C. Abraham has been appointed Moderator's Commissary until a new Bishop is elected. He very ably chaired the biennial Diocesan Council in October and was also the Chief Guest at our Nurses' Graduation function in November.

We have had a variety of visitors during 1993. Dr Julian Stowell, the grandson of Rev. Frederick Stowell, cut the ribbon over the doorway of the new School of Nursing classroom block on 26 February, the hospital's 80th anniversary. Rev. Stowell supervised the building of the hospital in 1911–12 during the furlough of Rickard Hickling. It was good to continue the link with the family. Louise Isager, a pre-nurse student from Denmark unveiled the stone plaque inside the doorway—another link with the past as the former Danish missionary Lisbeth Morch was Nursing Superintendent and Principal of the School of Nursing from 1929 to 1959. We also had a visit from Margaret Jones and her husband, son and daughter-in-law. After serving 16 years in Jammalamadugu Hospital, her father Dr T.T. Thomson was Medical Superintendent in Chickballapur from 1922 to 1932. So our links with the past continue.

We had our first American-born Indian medical student—Anand—spend some time with us. He was very interested in obstetrics and was so keep to make the most of his time here, even to the extent of sleeping in a side room of the maternity ward to be on hand for the many night deliveries. Arriving back at the bungalow in the early morning along with the newspaper boy, he earned the nickname 'Delivery Boy'!

We continue to repair and modernise staff houses, as well as put up new buildings. In 1993, we had the official opening of a new male private ward, donated by a local lawyer. This room, with attached toilet, bathroom and cooking space, is much appreciated by patients who are able to pay more for a private room where a relative can stay with them. Two of such private wards have had, however, to be turned into staff quarters while the houses were being repaired. We have space available in the hospital grounds, as well as land the size of a football field outside, where we could build new housing for staff if we had the funds. May we invite donations, please?

Some friends have already sent donations towards the School of Nursing classroom block, which is now in full use, with a garden blooming in the inner quadrangle and trees and bushes coming up along the front entrance. We are grateful too to those who have contributed towards the new Outpatient Dept. block now taking place.

At our weekly singsongs with the nurses and students in the past few weeks, we have been singing Christmas carols and tomorrow they meet in our bungalow to sing—and help eat up all the savouries and sweets presented to us over Christmas! The following chorus is a popular choice and we close with it as our belated Christmas and New Year wish to you all, that your lives may be blessed as ours are.

CHORUS: My life is really blessed because I know the love of God
            And I can be so free to live and move within that love.
            Part of His family, living in victory,
            Secure in knowing that Jesus has got everything in hand.

1.   Sometimes I wonder if I'll ever get through,
            And I see my life's in need of changing.
            But though He disciplines, it's always in love,
            And so with confidence I say…

CHORUS:
2.   So I'm really happy to be walking with God,
            Knowing His care from day to day;
            He is the answer to my every desire,
            And so with confidence I say…

CHORUS: My life is really blessed because I know the love of God
            And I can be so free to live and move within that love;
            Part of His family, living in victory,
            Secure in knowing that Jesus has got everything in hand.

Betty and Leslie

Letter 31
New Outpatient Department.
Leprosy Patient

Cowdenbeath

18 October 1994

Dear Friends,

Writing this during our furlough while based with Betty's sister in Cowdenbeath. We have been able to meet some of you and speak to others on the phone, but time is all too short, as was our twelve days' holiday in the south of Skye, blessed as it was with glorious weather.

The highlight of the past year in Chickballapur has been the completion of the new Outpatient Department. When we first saw the architect's drawings it seemed a complicated structure but it has become a very beautiful building in which a large part of our daily work can be done in a supportive environment. It accommodates all the doctors' clinics (9 doctors and a dentist), pharmacy, laboratory, x-ray and treatment rooms in a circle around a central open space where the patients wait under the shelter of a fibreglass roof.

Who are these patients? They are people with fever, or pains, or ulcers or people who think they need an operation for a hernia or a prolapse or for a tubectomy for family planning. They may be people coming back for a check-up after an operation or after some days in the hospital for typhoid or tuberculosis or maybe just someone with depression in one of its many manifestations.

However, there are many others outside who are sick, who could be helped by medicines if only they could reach help. Some do not know they could be helped. Some cannot afford the money or the time to come to a hospital. Some do not know that they have early stages of a disease that could be cured. In this latter category are many with tuberculosis or leprosy.

In India at present, the government is organising the resources for the eradication of leprosy by the year 2000. To do this it is necessary to find all those infected with leprosy that may not be aware of their condition. This means a search of all the population—a gigantic if not impossible task. Our hospital has been given the care of all the people in the Chickballapur area (about 160,000). We go out monthly to eight distribution centres to give tablets to the patients who have been diagnosed and to check on their progress.

For nine months, Narayana met us once a month when we stopped at the entrance to his village. He was an eight-year-old who was found during a survey of all the children in the village school. A school survey is one of the more economical ways of looking for undiagnosed patients who are only about one or two in every thousand inhabitants of a village. He did not know anything about the pale patch in the middle of his back—probably never saw it—but our leprosy supervisor recognised a leprosy patch and treatment was started. Eight months' treatment is the minimum for this type of leprosy but the patch was still faintly visible at the end of six months and a further three months' treatment was given just to make sure that he was cured. Our leprosy workers will now check him again after six months in case any signs of the disease reappears.

We treat many children and young people with small patches like Narayana's. One such was Muninarsasimhaiah, a Christmas day baby born 18 years ago in our hospital! His mother was a village girl with very low intelligence—so low that her next child was born by the roadside without help and rescued by our staff, taking mother and child to the hospital. His father was a leprosy patient who first realised something was wrong when he found the skin wearing off his fingers as he pulled the rope to bring a bucket of water up from the well. His fingers were terribly ulcerated but there was no pain! He was brought to the hospital and treatment started. The leprosy is now cured but the damaged bits of his fingers and toes cannot be replaced and the nerve damage means that he must be ever careful to prevent new ulcers on his hands and feet. He wears protective foam rubber sandals provided by the hospital, and he lives on the hospital compound where he does light work, collecting the bits of paper and plastic bags etc., which people scatter all over the hospital compound. He uses a special tool like a spring rake to do this work and protect his hands. He has attended the services in our hospital chapel and has been baptised, changing his name to Enoch. He only gets a small salary but he has spent much of that on educating the one son, Muninarsasimhaiah, now renamed Yesu Prasad (Gift of Jesus).

Yesu Prasad has completed the twelve years of schooling and was recently accepted for training as a Ward Assistant in the hospital. This will be a three months' course that will equip him to carry out the simpler nursing duties in the wards. He may go on later for the leprosy programme and thus play his part in eradicating the disease, which has crippled his father and mildly afflicted him at one time.

We watched the T.V. programme showing Anika Rice moving the Accident and Emergency Unit from Dunfermline to Romania. We had a similar experience in our hospital when a complete dental unit was shipped from Germany to Madras by courtesy of kind friends in Germany. We did not have Anika's team of workers though to get it from Madras to our hospital. The equipment came in large wooden crates on a lorry and a team of hospital workers helped to break open the crates and unload the various pieces. Our dental clinic room in the new Outpatient Dept. was not ready for use when the equipment arrived but we installed things in the old operation theatre temporarily. Lesley Porteous, a dentist from Edinburgh, came to India with us when we returned in November 1992, to spend a year in our hospital. She was able to use some of the equipment while she was with us. After some time we were able to appoint an Indian dentist, Dr Afsal, a Muslim, and he turned up unexpectedly on the day engineers came from Bangalore to install things in the new building. Well-timed! Now the dental dept. is fully functioning and Dr Afsal has been visiting schools and colleges in Chickballapur examining children and calling in those who require dental treatment. Much work needs to be done in dental health in India. Many have beautiful pearly white teeth but many more adults have terribly rotten teeth through chewing betel nut, often mixed with tobacco, and causing quite a few to suffer from mouth cancer.

The syllabus for the three-year nursing training gives much importance to community health and as the student nurses go round the villages visiting homes and schools they give training on health care including care of the teeth and also examining for leprosy.

Betty has spent a lot of time during this past year house hunting for staff quarters and a place where the student nurses could stay to be easily accessible for calls for home deliveries. Mr Michael Yesupriya, a member of our local church, added a first floor to his house in the poorer part of Chickballapur and we were able to rent the two small flats there for the use of staff and students. Sister Liz, a qualified Community Health Nurse-midwife from Cambridge spent a year with us as a volunteer and was able to get this work set up, then handed it over to Sister Grace, one of our Senior Staff Nurses in the hospital. Two student nurses spend two weeks at a time staying with Grace, living together as a family with a volunteer doctor living next door. They go out daily on home visits of pregnant women and for postnatal check-ups. They conduct home deliveries and run thrice weekly clinics in a small room (old vestry of a now ruined church building) nearby. This service is now much appreciated by the village women, although at first not many women were willing to be examined by the nurse or students. Difficult cases are referred to our hospital but careful monitoring and check-ups during pregnancy are helping to prevent miscarriages or late arrival at the hospital, resulting in complicated labour or fits etc.

Dr Prema our gynaecologist/obstetrician continues to be very busy in our maternity department, with over 120 deliveries per month, many of which are complicated and requiring Caesarean sections or forceps deliveries. Now, with a paediatrician on the staff, Dr Venkatachalapathy, a local young man, our children's wards are filling up, and the sick babies in the delivery ward have expert care to help them recover fully. Many of the mothers in the maternity ward come to our hospital 'shop' to buy clothes for their new-born as it is not the custom to prepare layettes beforehand. It is considered to be tempting the devil for an expectant mother to be making any preparations. Often the new-born babe is wrapped in a piece of cloth until the father or other relative goes out to buy clothes. We have a stock of nice hand-knitted bonnets, jackets and bootees on sale in the outpatient department, donated by kind friends in the UK These sales help the babies and the funds go towards buying equipment for the hospital. We are grateful to all those who have sent such gifts during the past year. Unfortunately, some parcels did not reach us and one HUGE parcel attracted the attention of customs officials and much duty had to be paid, later reimbursed by the group that sent the parcel. From time to time, we have fundraising events, sales both in the hospital and in Bangalore. Most of the time a cupboard in the injection room is our 'shop' with biscuits, sweets and other eatables kept there, and packets or bottles of juice in the fridge, alongside the injections. On special occasions, a table in the centre of the new O.P.D. is a good place to show our wares. Homemade birthday cards, Christmas cards, and calendars printed with the hospital name are good sellers.

We are returning again soon to our busy home in Chickballapur, 5 November, which is at present being cared for by Sister Margaret Kelly, a Senior Nurse from Kinross in Scotland, who is visiting us for the third time, and helping the Nursing Superintendent as well as caring for visitors in the bungalow. There

174

are many visitors there from the UK and elsewhere, some for just a few hours, some staying for up to a year, who give very useful help with the work in the hospital or in the Community Health Department.

We go back to the preparations for Christmas and probably also the opening of the new church—a very imposing and grand building, complete with a large bell at the top of one of its two towers. Hopefully, we may soon have a new Bishop for our diocese also.

Betty and Leslie

Letter 32
Betty Patient Colles Fracture

Chickballapur
1 November 1995

Dear Friends,

Greetings to everyone on this Festival Day—Karnataka Day. Formerly known as Mysore State, it was renamed as Karnataka State on 1 November 1981. Today is a Public Holiday and the Outpatient Department is closed except for emergencies. Leslie and a volunteer Irish lady doctor from Edinburgh are 'on call' after going round the wards in the morning as all the other doctors are on leave for the festival.

Betty is resting with her left leg up on a stool after falling off her cycle into a drain in the hospital and giving herself a nasty gash on the shinbone! On the hospital's 82nd anniversary—26 February—after getting ready for a Thanksgiving Service in the circular seating area of our new Outpatient Department, Betty slipped on the newly polished tiled floor and suffered an incomplete Colles fracture of her left wrist! That slowed her down a bit, as there was no cycling for a few weeks and no typing for a time. Typing on the electronic typewriter at home depends on the availability of electricity, and this has been very erratic in recent months with power cuts for hours at a time. (Halfway through that sentence there was yet another power cut!)

Since Bishop Jathanna retired in July 1993, this Diocese has had a series of 'stand-in' Bishops appointed by the Moderator of the Church of South India who himself took charge for a time. We started with Dr K.C. Abraham and after several Bishops from other Dioceses, we now have the newest Bishop in C.S.I.— Rt. Rev. G.T. Abraham. He was installed as Bishop in Nandyal Diocese in October last year. He was ordained in June 1966 in Gooty where Betty was appointed in September 1966. He was her first Pastor and the one who gave her her first lesson in Telugu.

She had him speaking on her tape-recorder reciting the Lord's Prayer in Telugu, which she then learned by heart and continues to recite in the Kannada services in Chickballapur. Betty attended the Diocesan Council last week in Bangalore with Bishop Abraham as Chairman. Under his leadership, the meetings went on peacefully though we heard that much canvassing had gone on for election to posts and committees. During many of the sessions, comments were made about the need for a Bishop of our own, and hopefully, Synod will decide soon after the Synod meetings in January 1996. In the meantime, we are happy to have Bishop Abraham looking after us. He comes to Chickballapur on 25 November for the Hospital Board meeting, followed by a Confirmation Service in the Church on 26 November. Over 50 young people are attending Confirmation classes at present. During the year, a group of 60 were confirmed, so this is encouraging. Our pastor Rev. Sathyanandam Paul has also been persuading many families who have not been legally married to come forward for a short simple service either in his house or in the church.

More and more in recent years, we are seeing western customs creeping into India and many magazines brought into the bungalow by volunteers and visitors have to be vetted before being left around, as both articles and pictures give bad examples of western habits these days!

While we are enjoying worshipping in a new church building, just one year old (dedicated and opened on 11 December 1994) recently we attended the 175th anniversary of Memorial Church in Bangalore, which Leslie attended when he was based in Bangalore from 1962 to 1966. This is a Tamil speaking congregation and Leslie was encouraged to join in the singing of Tamil lyrics when he was studying Tamil at the language school. He also played the organ there. As a memento of the 175th anniversary, a mounted laminated photo of the church with a quartz clock in the corner was presented to him and other elders and office-bearers.

Another special occasion in the family was the final profession of Sister Rosemary as a nun in the Roman Catholic Church. She is the sister of our cook Jayasheela. She was one of 12 nuns being received that day. The convent auditorium was decorated with large paper sunflowers and the text, "We ever turn to seek you, Lord." The nuns came in procession carrying a single real sunflower, which they placed in a pot in front of the altar. In many parts of

Karnataka fields of sunflowers can be found, grown for the oil in the seed. On a sunny day, it is quite a sight to see the large flowers turning to the sun.

The other day many of us were fascinated to look through special goggles at the solar eclipse. In this part of India, it was only partial but what we did see was an amazing sight. The television broadcast showed scenes from various spots in North India where the full eclipse was visible, and where groups from around the world were carrying out various scientific tests. Many people, however, in this part still feared this unusual event, remained indoors, and would not eat during the eclipse.

Officially, we have two male junior and two female junior doctors, a paediatrician, an orthopaedic surgeon, a junior gynaecologist, a part-time obstetrician/gynaecologist and a part-time E.N.T. and eye surgeon and Leslie. One day during September, Dr Pauline and Leslie were the only two doctors in the hospital! We have over 200 in-patients and about 150 outpatients per day! That was just a one-day 'crisis' but one junior lady doctor left recently to join her husband in the US and another has given notice of her resignation. The search is on for more junior doctors. Any volunteers from the UK who would like to come for six months or a year? We have advertised in a Christian newspaper for not only junior doctors, but for an anaesthetist, a physician and a general surgeon.

We now have all our present volunteers knitting squares, and our third blanket is nearly finished. We can't say the same about the construction work on the buildings. Instead of getting the roof on, workmen are now digging deep holes for pillars to form the connecting corridor to the maternity ward. A new labour ward too has come to a standstill. There have been several Festival holidays in October and 1 November is a holiday, so that may be one of the reasons for the lack of workmen.

Betty has been out and about house-hunting again for staff quarters. The owner of one house, which the hospital had rented, wanted her house back. Three houses were tracked down and negotiations with the owners took place. One house is beautiful but the owner is asking for a large amount as lease. Rs. 2 lakhs (about £4,000). Leasing is the way people are letting their houses. They can use the money to pay off their debts, or invest it in the bank. After the lease period is over the amount is returned to us. We have to calculate how much interest we could get if we put the money in the bank and that then works out at the equivalent of a rent per month. The other alternative is for us to build a new house ourselves in the hospital compound where there is plenty of room to build.

However, that would take time and we need a house urgently for the dental doctor.

One never knows from day to day what crisis will turn up next. We press on and things work out in the end if we don't panic. We often have power cuts. Some are for the repair of lines, and power is soon restored. Now, after more than a week of power-cuts lasting for several hours (4 pm to 2 am the other day), we now read in the newspaper that there are to be regular power cuts for the next seven months because of the failure of monsoon rains in the catchment areas!

As we buy and sell greeting cards for Christmas this year, we have cards from an organisation called CRY (Child Relief and You). We too have a slogan to help raise funds for our various projects: CSI Hospital Chickballapur, "Contribute Something to Improve the Health of Children!" We thank all those who continue to support us with their prayers, their gifts of baby clothes, knitted blankets, donations towards new buildings, old greeting cards etc. A big THANK YOU to all!

Tonight at our weekly singsong with the staff and student nurses, we are going to try singing a new *Song for the Nations* that we heard sung at the Memorial Church anniversary. We think it would be an appropriate theme song for the nurses' graduation service and also an appropriate thought as we come near to the end of the year. We end this newsletter with the words of this hymn.

Song for the Nations.

May we be a shining light to the nations
A shining light to the peoples of the earth
Till the whole world sees the glory of Your name
May your pure light shine through us.

> May we bring a word of hope to the nations
> A word of life to the peoples of the earth
> Till the whole world knows
> There's salvation through Your name
> May your mercy flow through us.

May we be a healing balm to the peoples of the earth
A healing balm to the peoples of the earth

Till the whole world knows the power of Your name
May your healing flow through us.

> May we sing a song of joy to the nations
> A song of praise to the peoples of the earth
> Till the whole world rings
> With the praises of your name
> May your song be sung through us.

May your kingdom come to the nations
Your will be done in the peoples of the earth
Till the whole world knows that Jesus Christ is Lord
May your kingdom come in us.
May your kingdom come on earth.

May the peace and joy of Christmas enrich your life and continue to bless you in 1996.

Betty and Leslie

Letter 33
Furlough September/October.
Leslie Patient Varicose Ulcers

Cowdenbeath
1 November 1996

Dear friends,

Greetings to you all from Scotland, where we are now in the last week of our furlough. We came home on 28 August and seem to have been on the go for most of these two months—travelling from Aberdeen to Exeter, with two trips to London. Maybe we had better start with the second of these trips, perhaps the highlight of this furlough—Leslie's visit to Buckingham Palace for the investiture for the O.B.E. News of this first came at the end of 1995 but was only announced in the New Year's Honours List, and as it was in the overseas list most of our friends missed this until the news spread along the grapevine. Leslie and Betty, along with Leslie's two sisters, Moira and Frances, were in the Palace for the Investiture. The ladies—Betty in a purple sari—were seated at the side of the ballroom with the band playing soft music while the Queen distributed the honours to each person. Leslie along with the other recipients was kept in the Picture Gallery until it was time to receive his medal. There were beautiful pictures and sculptures all over the place. Leslie stepped up before the Queen who pinned on his O.B.E. medal and asked a few questions. Immediately the last medal was given, the proceedings finished with the National Anthem and we all trooped out through the beautiful corridors of Buckingham Palace to the forecourt and our own photographs. No royal eats! Our family went off for a sumptuous Chinese meal with chopsticks in Chinatown before Moira and husband Richard hurried off to pack for a month's tour of Hawaii and Australia.

Forward planning for this furlough was hindered by the fact that Leslie had a varicose ulcer on his left ankle for some months and felt that an operation was required. While attending a church in Dunfermline we met an Indian Christian who is a General Surgeon at the Queen Margaret Hospital in Dunfermline, and he arranged for the operation to be done for varicose veins on both legs on 26 September. Leslie was admitted in the morning of the operation and discharged the next midday. All went well and already the varicose ulcer has healed, after some days rest and plenty of walks to encourage circulation.

On our first visit to London, several former visitors/volunteers met up with us at Livingstone House and on 20 September about 250 attended the annual gathering of Friends of the Church in India. Bishop Lesslie Newbigin and his wife who had recently celebrated their diamond wedding were there and many other Indian and missionary colleagues.

Highlights of the year in Chickballapur.

The new Outpatient Department has continued to bring inestimable benefits to our work with outpatients. Each room has been fully utilised with the Physiotherapy Department now also established there. Unfortunately, we still await a new x-ray machine for the x-ray room. The number of inpatients has increased much in recent months—officially 175 beds but reaching 230 some days in August this year.

The Maternity Department under the guidance of Dr Prema, Gynaecologist, has been exceptionally busy with up to 80 patients in the wards at one time. General and private wards have been packed with extra beds in all the corridors and up the middle of the ward. The labour ward had two beds so that two deliveries could be conducted simultaneously but in recent months there have been some days when three or four women were in labour at the same time, and the extra ones have been delivered in the corridor outside the labour room or in the room kept for eclamptic patients.

Seeing this situation, a wealthy landowner from a village 3 km from Chickballapur offered to build an extension to our present labour ward if we equipped it ourselves. The building has gone on slowly—not helped by the original contractor running off with the advance he was paid for the building. However, we understand that this building will be ready for use when we return to India, along with the six double and four single wards for women patients. This was built between the existing Maternity Ward and Women's General Ward and provides a covered way so that patients can be wheeled on a trolley from the Maternity Ward to the Operation Theatre without being exposed to the heavy rains in the monsoon season. The private wards will provide some more income, which will enable us to provide free treatment for the very poor and replace some of our old equipment in the wards and laboratory.

For much of this year, we have been short of junior doctors and Leslie has been kept busier than ever in the operating theatre, seeing the patients in the clinics and in the wards and being on call every second night for new admissions for some weeks. We were very glad to have had volunteer doctors from the UK— Alex, Pauline and Mary, and they were very helpful in the clinics, ward rounds, community health and in taking classes for the student nurses.

The bungalow has overflowed several times this year with some of our visitors or volunteers being boarded out in other houses in the hospital compound or in rented homes nearby. Our biggest number at one time was 12, but our cook Jayasheela and her husband Muthu (assistant cook in the nurses' hostel) and her sister Arita and brother's wife Raji coped with cooking for our increased family.

Two kittens were added to the family in January—Sheba and Shona. Several cat-loving volunteers recommend we have a cat for company when we felt lonely—or to help keep down the mice population in the kitchen and back veranda.

Betty has been kept busy proof-reading and arranging for the printing and publishing of a book *Jackfruit and Wild Honey* by Barbara Graham, widow of the late Dr Keith Graham who was Medical Superintendent in Chickballapur before Leslie took over in 1968. It tells of the life of Mr E. R. Sabapathy, Leprosy Social Worker in the hospital, and recounts tales of his work in the villages around. It was hoped to have the book ready for selling during our furlough, but unfortunately, it was delayed. There will be more news of this later when it is available. The book is illustrated by line drawings by Gregor, son of Dr and Mrs Graham.

We were happy to receive a copy of Gwen Morris's little biography, GO EAST YOUNG WOMAN, which tells of her beginnings in London, work in China as a missionary and from there to India where was she was a colleague of Betty in the Rayalaseema Diocese, Andhra Pradesh. Like so many other missionary colleagues (many of whom we met at the Friends of the Church in India gathering in London on 20 September) Gwen kept busy in London for quite a few years after her retirement.

As we start to pack our suitcases for return to India on 6 November, we think back over the past nine weeks in the UK and wish we had been able to fit in more visits during our furlough. We did manage a trip to Aberdeen while staying with a niece in Banchory and shared in a service in Danestone and Balmedie churches where Andy Cowie is the pastor. It was encouraging to see so many children at these services and to hear of their share in fundraising for the hospital. We were also able to visit Cumnock Church where many in the Congregation and youth organisations helped to raise funds for us.

At the Annual Assembly of the Congregational Federation (held for the first time in Scotland in the Methodist Central Hall, Edinburgh), some of the children were there to present us with a large 2 ft. x 3 ft. Bank of Scotland cheque for £4,484.56p towards the purchase of a much needed new ambulance for the hospital. Further donations have since been added to this amount to bring the total to £5,000. We look forward to placing an order for a new Tempo Trax vehicle when we return to India, to replace the larger Mahindra ambulance, which is badly in need of major repair.

We also shared with many friends at the Scottish Congregational Assembly at St Andrews early in September and at individual churches, especially Dunfermline, during our short stay. We are thankful to them all for their fellowship and continued help.

While in Aberdeen, we were interviewed for a Christian Radio programme, which went on the air on 20 October—the start of ONE WORLD WEEK. In this, we mentioned the gift for the new ambulance and said that our next need was for an ultrasound scan machine. The children in Aberdeen have already started fundraising for this but at a cost of approx. £9,000, we need help from many others so that this piece of equipment can be installed in the hospital.

We arrived in Edinburgh on 29 August and will leave from there on 6 November, flying to Amsterdam, Bombay and Bangalore, in time for a farewell function for Dr Hymavathi who retires as Medical Supt. of C.S.I. Hospital, Bangalore. At present, the E.N.T. doctor is acting as Med. Supt. but the appointment of a new successor has yet to be made. We had hoped that during interviews for the hospital we might have been able to find an Asst. Medical Supt. for Chickballapur who could share some of the responsibilities and perhaps take over when we retire in 1999. We could do with the help of a senior doctor/surgeon/administrator.

A new auditor, auditing the hospital accounts this year was amazed at the size of the accounts, which had all been done by hand without the aid of a computer. This is a piece of equipment, which would ease the work in the Administration Dept.—accounts, salaries, pharmacy stock etc. With regular power-cuts for five hours each day (10 am to 3 pm) for most of this year, plus erratic fluctuations (160 volts–300 volts instead of a steady 240 volts) in the supply when it IS there, we need our new 30 kva diesel generator to be on for about 6 hours every day—burning up expensive diesel—and additional stabilisers to cope with the surges in power.

Betty and Leslie

Letter 34
Visitors, May and Grace, Barbara Graham. Betty Broken Ankle

Chickballapur
14 November 1997

Dear Friends,

Our hospital Christmas card for this year is a group of hospital staff children wearing brightly coloured striped sweaters knitted by women in a church in Birmingham. From time to time, they send us parcels of these woollens, which we sell in aid of hospital funds. We took snaps of the front and back view of the group of children and thought it would make an interesting and unusual card! We had 2,000 cards printed so hope for good sales to help our fundraising.

Having completed the block of private wards, which were opened on 6 February, we are now seeking to raise funds for an ultrasound scan machine. Four doctors from Bangalore continue to come one Sunday each with their own portable scan machine. Between 30-40 patients, mostly pregnant women, but others also, come for this diagnostic procedure. If we had our own machine, the patients could be seen at any time.

The Senior Partner in a group practice in England ran in a mini-marathon and raised £1,202 from her sponsors and other events. Her partner, Dr Alex Ladha who had worked with us as a volunteer, came back to visit us in October bringing this contribution. It was good to have him back albeit for only a few days along with Jane Barbour a nurse in the Western General Hospital, Edinburgh. Jane had also worked as a volunteer with us. We always enjoy return visits from former medical students and other volunteers.

We hear of another means of Scan fundraising—by connecting the dots on an outline of a baby—supposedly, as it appears on a scan! We hope the young people in the Scottish Congregational Federation do well with their fundraising by this means—ten pence from dot to dot and each baby raises £5.

We mentioned return visits from students and volunteers. We have had several of these during the year. A medical student from Wales who had been here in 1975, now a Consultant Cardiologist in London, came for the day while taking part with another English cardiologist working with the Heart Foundation in Manipal Hospital, Bangalore. He was interested to see the changes and many new buildings in the hospital since his last visit.

Louise Isager, a pre-nursing student from Denmark—following in the footsteps, we thought, of Sister Lisbeth Morch, former Missionary Nursing Superintendent from Denmark—spent six months in our maternity ward a few years ago, before starting nursing training in Denmark. However, she then decided to study medicine instead and came back to see us for a few days along with her younger sister who is training to be a nurse!

Barbara Graham, who wrote the book, *Jackfruit and Wild Honey* about our former leprosy worker, Mr E. R. Sabapathy, is back in India. She spent a few days in Chickballapur with her daughter Fiona and her granddaughters Sarah and Katy. Barbara will be in India until mid-January and will be back to stay longer with us after the other three return to Australia after a ten-day whirlwind tour of South India.

Another of our fundraising items here in Chickballapur is friendship bracelets. Jennifer, a medical student from Dundee University taught us how to make these colourful wristbands with wool or embroidery threads. Our cook Jayasheela then worked out even more elaborate diamond designs, which we are selling in the hospital. We are taking orders with colour requests! We made special orange, white and green—the colours of India's national flag—for Independence celebrations in August.

Grace Dunlop who sends out these Christmas circular letters for us had visited Betty in Andhra Pradesh in 1975. She came back with Betty's sister May Scott for three weeks in October. Betty went with them on a tour of her old haunts in the Rayalaseema Diocese—Anantapur, Gooty, Nandikotkur, Nandyal, Jammalamadugu, Muddanur, Kamalapuram, Cuddapah and Madanapalle—a 3-day 895 km. tour in the hospital jeep—the new Tempo Trax vehicle, which we had taken delivery of in January. The roads varied immensely from National Highway wide 4-lane smooth tarred roads, to roads with only room for 1½ cars necessitating two passing vehicles having to move to the rough sides of the road.

Most drivers waited until the last moment before giving way—much to the consternation of May and Grace! Flashing headlights mean I AM COMING—MAKE WAY. The constant blaring of horns, and headlights on full beam at night, animals all over the place, and road diversions through fields, all added to the strain of road travel in India.

Our visitors also experienced different kinds of trains. We went to New Delhi by the new select Rajdhani air-conditioned train. Again Betty accompanied Grace and May on this 6-day trip, enjoying the comfort and service of this train. Newspapers, bottled water, coffee, snacks, meals and bedding were all supplied on the 36-hour journey. On the return from Agra, after seeing the Taj Mahal, we travelled on an ordinary express train and although it was First Class there was no air-conditioning, no bed-roll, and at first no bed, although we had been allotted bed space. Two men in our compartment volunteered to sleep on the floor between the two bunks on either side. The fans in the compartment blew hot air around and wafted through the open windows but we survived the trip nevertheless! We came back from an overnight visit to Mysore to the sad news of the sudden death of Sister Joyce Woollard, an English missionary colleague, in CMC Hospital, Vellore.

Joyce had had a fall in February and cracked her femur. On 2 March, it fractured, and she had a total hip replacement in Bangalore. She then had a series of operations, in May was transferred to Vellore, and was just beginning to walk when other complications set in—pneumonia, hepatitis B, infected right hip joint, septicaemia, breathing problem, and she became semi-conscious. She eventually passed away on 24 October and her body was brought to Vishranthi Nilayam where she had been Warden for eight years. A very moving service was held in St Mark's Cathedral before she was laid to rest in Hosur Road Cemetery, Bangalore. A Service of Thanksgiving is being held on the 40th day at Vishranthi Nilayam after which the new guest room building is being opened and named in her memory—Wednesday, 3 December.

Betty's mother also passed away on 23 June, after a fall while in hospital, without ever regaining consciousness. She would have been 89 in December and had had a good life until a few years ago when she suffered a stroke and gradually became less able to walk. On the day of her cremation in Scotland, we held a service in our hospital chapel with over 100 staff and student nurses attending. It was comforting to have the support of our hospital family, as we could not be with May and the rest of the family at the crematorium.

The news of the sudden death of Princess Diana and Dodi in a car accident in August was another sad event that affected many people around the world, including us here in Chickballapur. Then came the death of Mother Teresa on the day of Diana's funeral. As Queen Elizabeth referred a few years ago to her 'annus horribilis'—Betty—a.k.a. Elizabeth R. if she wants to use her full name— also felt she had had a bad year.

On 18 May, Betty had a fall—slipped between the step in front of the Outpatient Department and the jeep—twisted her ankle and broke three bones (typical Pott's fracture plus a third fracture). Leslie twisted the ankle back into place and the next day the Orthopaedic surgeon in a three-hour operation, put in a metal plate and screws on one bone and two long screws in the other. Betty was able to 'enjoy' the comfort of one of the new female private wards, which had been opened in February. After a week in the hospital, she was allowed home for another week's rest in bed, and then was up and about in a wheelchair then walking frame, then elbow crutches. The bones healed very well and now only a tight elastic stocking gives some support.

We celebrated Betty's 60th birthday in March with a few days' holiday, at our honeymoon hotel in Mahabalipuram. On our return, we decided that we should advertise for a local person to be a Personal Assistant to the Medical Superintendent (Betty's job until now), who would get to know the routine of the office before the new Med. Supt. takes over from Leslie who is due to retire in March 1999. After advertising and two sets of interviews, Miss Kumari was appointed and joined on 4 October. She is slowly taking over new work while Betty attempts to clear a backlog of papers and files.

While celebrating the hospital's 84th anniversary on 26 February, Rev. S. Vasanthakumar was consecrated as Bishop of our Karnataka Central Diocese in St Mark's Cathedral, Bangalore. As the Church of South India, as well as the Republic of India, celebrates 50 years, various events have been held both locally and in Madras. In May, each year, the transfers of pastors in the diocese take place, usually after five years in one place, and so CSI Christ Church, Chickballapur had a change of presbyter with Rev. Arunkumar Wesley appointed here. Betty went with him and others from the diocese to attend the Synod Jubilee celebrations in Madras. A huge marquee was erected on the grounds of St George's Cathedral and many white-haired former missionaries could be seen in the 4,000+ gathering.

In the hospital during the year, much new building and repair work has been completed. On our return from 2½ months' furlough in the UK on 6 November 1996, we had the opening of the watchman's room at the entrance to the hospital; then the much-needed 4-bedded labour room attached to the maternity ward, which had been donated and built by a local well-wisher. The long-awaited block of new private wards was opened on 6 February with the first donor Narayanamma being traditionally presented with a shawl and a garland of flowers as a token of appreciation and thanks. Her photograph hangs in Room 1, with a stone plaque outside the door. It is appropriate that today, Nehru's birthday (celebrated as Children's Day in India), saw Narayanamma's granddaughter deliver twins (a boy and a girl) and be put in her room! Narayanamma was all smiles as she proudly showed off her great-grandchildren.

Three new staff houses were constructed in the hospital compound and two wards altered and repaired to provide accommodation for eight staff nurses. Other staff quarters are in need of repair, and there are always more requests for accommodation than we can provide.

In April, we were able to purchase a computer and already we are finding how useful this piece of equipment is. At first salaries and financial statements were the main items put into the computer. Over the past few months our Office Manager, Cecil Daniel, has been producing a variety of reports and papers including today, the programme for the School of Nursing Graduation and Lamp Lighting Ceremony to be held on 29 November. Nineteen nurses have completed their three years of general nursing and midwifery training and now receive their badges, certificates and have a black stripe added to their caps. Nineteen new students joined the course on 1 July and, having now completed and passed the preliminary training period, were given caps.

With email bringing fast communication worldwide, we hope that we too may soon be able to link our computer to the Internet and be connected instantly with many of you around the world. Many of the medical students who apply to us give an email address. To be able to order pharmacy supplies and other hospital requirements with records of stock on the computer, will be a great help in future. Another computer for the pharmacy records is next on our list of needs!

Looking back, the year has not been so bad after all. We have had our ups as well as downs. There have been encouraging events, as well as disappointing times. Some members of staff have left, but new ones have joined us. As we look forward to celebrating the hospital's 85th Anniversary in February 1998, we give thanks for all that has gone before and go forward into the unknown in faith and trust.

Betty and Leslie

Letter 35
Leslie Varicose Ulcers, Visitors

Chickballapur
22 October 1998

Dear Friends,

Let's light a candle for Christmas,
A symbol of joy and good cheer,
And then keep it bright in the window
And in our lives all through the year.

Let's light a candle with all of our warmth
Our friendship and love and goodwill
So that even when Christmas is over,
Its meaning will be shining still.

(Constance Parker Graham)

These are the words we have had printed on our hospital Christmas cards for this year. Usually, we cut up old cards and stick these onto the locally printed card. As well as continuing to do this, we also decided to make cards with photographs of children, patients, staff and buildings. Sandra McIntyre, a former volunteer with Scottish World Exchange, has returned for the third time on her own and has been busy taking photographs around the hospital. As this will be our last Christmas in India, we also decided to produce a 12-page calendar with photographs and plan to send parcels of these to the UK. The calendar will be a daily reminder of the people here as we settle back into life in Scotland on retirement in April 1999.

We are grateful to Paul C. Dass of Provision India for his work on the calendar, helping us choose the right photographs, designing the front cover and choosing the texts and script type etc. With the help of the printer's latest computer, Paul has created a really super calendar for us. We hope all who buy one will enjoy it as much as we have in creating it.

The Christian Medical Association of India had as its theme for Hospital Sunday and the Biennial Conference this month, SHALOM—Health and Peace—and had a picture of a fluffy yellow chicken being held in cupped hands. We decided to have this design printed on T-shirts for the hospital's anniversary and sold them to staff and supporters of the hospital.

As we did on a previous anniversary (80th), we organised a cycle race from the hospital to a village 12 km away. All contestants wore the special T-shirts and as we cycled through the town ringing cycle bells, we attracted much attention. This event was filmed by Sandra on her camcorder as she sat on the back of a scooter, sometimes sitting backwards to see the cyclists!

Betty writes: In May 1987, I fell outside the entrance to the Outpatient Department and fractured my right ankle in three places. Slowly during the year, the ankle healed and I was able to walk and cycle, though not rushing around as much as before. During my spell in the hospital and limited exercise for several months, I had put on over 15 kg. in weight and have never been able to lose it. When I was in hospital again to remove the metal plate, Nadia, a medical student from Switzerland kept an eye on my diet and limited the portions and selection of items! At the same time, I heard from a former missionary colleague, Peggy Hawkings, now in New Zealand, of a FIT FOR LIFE DIET, which stipulated only fresh fruit till noon to clean out the system. So with plenty variety of fruit, especially papaya and guavas, sapota, custard apples, limes, apples and bananas (though these were restricted) I enjoyed my new healthy eating habits and managed to lose the 15 kg, which I had put on earlier. I am managing to keep my weight steady, even with special meals for birthdays, weddings, festivals etc. from time to time.

To celebrate India's 50th Anniversary of Independence, one 5-star hotel in Bangalore—Le Meridian—had a special offer of a 50% reduction in meals during September. I enjoyed three meals there during the period of the special offer! In spite of this, I still managed to maintain my weight! As a child, I had been brought up on the adage, 'Don't let food go to waste' and was often persuaded to take a little extra to finish a dish etc. As my weight kept creeping up Leslie warned me, "Don't let food go to waist!" So I am now following this 'rule' and letting 'leftovers' go to the cats or buffalo!

After recovery from my ankle injury, and moving around normally, it was Leslie's turn to have a spell in bed. The varicose veins on both legs had developed ulcers, which were not healing, and when we were able to get a junior surgeon, Leslie was able to have rest in bed. We were grateful for the timely arrival of Dr Basavarajappa and his help for four months before he went for higher studies. In August, we were able to appoint Dr Konanahalle, a senior surgeon with ten years' experience in the UK, and a further ten years spending six months in India and six months in the UK. Since he joined, he has been doing most of the general surgery, with a few former patients still insisting on having only Leslie operate on them! Slowly Dr Konanahalle and Dr Krishnan are treating most of the new patients. The latter worked here for four years as a junior doctor after completing his training. He then went to the C.S.I. Holdsworth Memorial Hospital in Mysore for 18 years. Now, taking early retirement from there, he has re-joined our staff as a physician. With relatives in the area, he has settled back happily in Chickballapur. Leslie is now able to spend time in the mornings on hospital administration and paperwork etc. He sees patients in the clinic in the afternoons when there is an empty clinic. At present, we have three Consultants who have their own clinics at home in the afternoon and come only to the hospital in the mornings or on special calls.

We have been advertising in the newspaper for a Senior Administrator for the hospital as we have been without one for some time now. Even with the help of computers, one in the Admin. Office and a new one being installed in the pharmacy and billing sections, much time is spent on the administration and maintenance of the hospital. We received several applications and hope that a suitable senior person with experience can take on these responsibilities to relieve Leslie.

The search is also on for the post of Medical Superintendent. The Diocesan Executive Committee is the appointing authority for heads of institutions in the diocese and only a Christian is eligible. It is a pity that the two doctors recently appointed are both Hindu and therefore not eligible.

During the year, we have had 83 visitors so far—with some medical students and volunteers staying for weeks and months—and some just for one or two days. Several during the year have been on repeat visits, and they have appreciated seeing the changes over the years since their last visit. Barbara

Graham from Australia, William and Margot Cutting dropped in on their world tour after retirement. Eileen Jacob retired and living in Hyderabad with her twin brother and his wife on holiday from England. While they were being shown around the hospital, we introduced them to a patient who had just deliver twins—a boy and a girl, so both sets of twins were happy to be photographed together. Rev. Charles Meachin and his wife Barbara came with a group of nine others from their church in England for the day. Another day we had three Indonesians attending an East Asian Women's Conference in Bangalore. It was good that Dr Anne Todman, daughter of Dr Rodney Todman who served here for some time, was able to pay a return visit with her doctor husband during the hospital's anniversary celebrations. They along with Betty took part in the cycle ride.

After having lived in this huge mission bungalow with four bedrooms, with attached bathrooms, large sitting room and dining room, kitchen, storeroom and wide front veranda, set in a huge compound with many large trees—mango, tamarind, fig, bamboo, eucalyptus and teak saplings (recently planted by the horticultural department)—we look forward to retiring to a much smaller house in Scotland. We hope friends will continue to visit us there, though preferably just one or two at a time!

This will be our last Christmas Newsletter from India and we are grateful to our friend Grace Dunlop for illustrating, duplicating and sending it out for us.

We are grateful to all those who have supported us and our work here over the past 30 years. Thanks to all who have written letters with news of events in their areas; for the many parcels of knitted goods, blankets, sweaters, teddy bears, fluffy toys etc. which we have received; donations towards our various projects over the years—our wedding ambulance, operation theatre equipment, outpatient department etc. Thank you one and all.

We look forward to our retirement and the opportunity to meet up with some of you again to give you first-hand news of the hospital.

For three days this week, we have been celebrating Diwali—the Festival of Lights—with firecrackers exploding all around us—as well as the colourful cascades of sparkles, Catherine wheels and sparklers etc. Soon children in the UK will be lighting bonfires with Guy Fawkes on top and then it will be time for the Christmas lights and decorations, which brings us back to the beginning of this letter and the candle poem.

So… Let's light a candle for Christmas,

A symbol of joy and good cheer.
And then keep it bright in the window
And in our lives all through the year...

Betty and Leslie

Letter 36
Leaving Chickballapur and Retirement
to Burnside, Rutherglen, Scotland

Rutherglen, Glasgow

28 September 1999

Dear Friends,

Having battled our way home from Church today in rain and gale force wind, we understand the hymn writer's *In the bleak midwinter*. It is a change from the warmth of India but we are getting accustomed to all the differences of life in Scotland since we arrived here at the end of April 1999. The weather has been kind to us so far. We still await our first snow but there has been frost after clear nights.

We look forward to our first Christmas in Scotland for many years and our first Christmas together in Scotland. (Betty says, "My last Christmas in Scotland was 1971 when I was on furlough for one year after spending five years in India.") It will certainly be a quieter Christmas this year. We will miss the carol singing in the wards and homes and the loss of sleep of the nights before Christmas this year, not to mention all the savouries and coffee enough to fill our stomachs and a plastic bag! We will have a service at 11:30 pm on Christmas Eve and another on Christmas morning with some of our family members. On 31 December, members of all the churches in this area are gathering at their respective churches and marching with flaming torches to a large church in the centre of the town as a Christian witness for the new millennium. This is one of the ways planned by the churches to usher in the year 2000.

After all the busyness of over 30 years in India, we are enjoying the rest and peace of Burnside. The last months in Chickballapur were most hectic—trying to clear up the accumulated contents of the Medical Superintendent's bungalow and office—papers and books that have been there for 60 years in some cases.

Unfortunately, all the functions and feasts, which were held during our last weeks in Chickballapur, left us without time to complete the task. How much the local people and hospital staff and others showered love and affection upon us. We were feasted well beyond our capacity to eat and we received so many gifts that we had to add three boxes to the luggage, which we sent to Scotland by ship. All 22 packages arrived safely in Scotland and have now been unpacked and arranged in our new home. These gifts make a daily reminder of our friends and colleagues in India, as well as adding beauty to our home. We soon realised that our house lacked adequate cupboard space so we had a fitted wardrobe and shelves put in our bedroom and more cupboards in the hallway so that a place could be found for everything.

Our home is near a large Safeway supermarket so shopping there was quite an adventure in the beginning. We were last in Scotland on furlough in September/October 1996, and we can see many changes in a variety of things since then, especially as we now have our own home and not living with relatives as we were used to on previous brief visits. Leslie's sister Frances, who lives a few streets away, had a meal ready for us when we arrived and had stocked the shelves and refrigerator with basic items of food. However, we soon had to see about more supplies. Firstly, we had to register at Safeway's to get an ABC card so that we could collect points when we shopped and thus give us a saving in future purchases. This was the first of many such cards, which we have since collected! Some are called Loyalty cards to encourage you to buy in that particular shop. From time to time, there are special offers and double points awarded to encourage you to buy even more from that shop. There are many charity shops and some of them too now have such cards. When negotiating the checkout point in Safeway's, twice I made the mistake of going to a counter, which was meant for nine items or less, and I had a trolley with about 20 items! I am amazed at the speed with which the shop assistant could check the various items, which have no price on them—simply a bar code—and her 'computer' knows, which items have been reduced or two for the price of one. Then instead of paying by cash, we present our bank debit card. I use this all the time in Safeway's and in most other shops when making big purchases. It saves carrying much cash, and most of the supermarkets will even give you cash if required. It still amuses me to be asked after every purchase, "Do you want any cashback?" Only once so far have I used this facility, but it saves going to the bank to cash a cheque or withdraw cash. Everywhere, not only outside a bank but also on other shops and office buildings can be seen, 'a hole in the wall' where cash can be taken on presenting your bank card.

Back to Safeway's and their special offers. From the beginning, I was attracted to their special counters with reduced items, bashed tins, damaged boxes etc. but also items that had a 'sell-by date' or 'use-by date' which was often that day, which meant that the item was supposed to be eaten that day. I could not resist many of these 'bargains' but then began to worry if I was likely to poison us if we ate things after the 'use by date'! Slowly I calmed down and stopped worrying but just used common sense as to whether it should be thrown out or could still be eaten. Not many things have had to be thrown out—but one thing I did discover was that bread often went mouldy within a few days. This reminded me of shopping in Bangalore for non-sweet bread and bringing extra loaves from there and finding that they went mouldy very quickly.

Comparing prices between the different sizes of packets and jars took time in the beginning when shopping and seeing such a variety of cereals, biscuits, bread, butter etc. Which ones to choose? Decisions, decisions all the time. Then other special offers of two for the price of one and being able to put the extra one in the deep freeze!

What other things took time to get used to—seeing buses and trains, shops and offices, with NO SMOKING signs? People were found standing smoking outside their office or shop or at bus stops. Now, we enjoy sitting upstairs in the local bus into Glasgow city centre. Formerly smoking was allowed upstairs in double-decker buses and the air could be quite thick so non-smokers usually avoided going upstairs if possible!

Why did we find so many large rubber bands on the pavements? We soon discovered that on some streets, there was a red box—often near a letterbox— and this was for the post office van to deliver piles of mail for that street or area, and the postman going on foot from door to door, would collect the mail, in bundles held together with a rubber band. No doubt, he ripped off the rubber band and let it drop. We have collected quite a few, as we don't like to see waste, and can use them!

We found it strange to see people walking along the street with their hand up at their ear talking—to themselves? No, they were talking into their mobile phones! It seems that it is not only businesspeople who need to be contactable at all times! While travelling by bus or train we have seen many mobiles phones in use. One young mother with three children on the coach from Glasgow to

London was constantly phoning her mother reporting on where they were and how the children were behaving—or not!

After the hectic few weeks sorting and packing and 'eating our way out of India', with invitations for breakfast, lunch and dinner etc., we were happy to be on our own, slowly unwinding when we first arrived here. Getting up a little later than we had been doing in India—7:30 am instead of 5:30 am—we enjoyed a leisurely breakfast while watching the news on television. Then a programme of interviews by Kilroy on a series of different problems in society, then a programme of patients and staff in a city hospital. That took us up to coffee time. Then a visit to the shops for food for lunch, back home and cook it in time to eat while watching the latest news. The weather, on the whole, was very good—warm and sunny—so many days found us making sandwiches and going out for a walk around nearby parks, visiting gardens, exhibitions etc. and enjoying a picnic lunch. As we are both now over 60 years of age, we qualify for special concessions on buses and trains and entry to exhibitions and entertainment programmes! We are enjoying all these to the full!

We have had several long-distance trips; in July to Birmingham and Selly Oak for the closing Thanksgiving Service at St Andrews Hall; in October to London for the annual gathering of the Friends of the Church in India; in November, again to London, for CWM's Thanksgiving Service and an opportunity to visit CWM's new headquarters in Ipalo House. We had other visits during the year, to York to visit Leslie's sister Moira and family; to Dunfermline to attend the funeral of a missionary friend; to Crieff for a memorial service for another friend who just missed his 90th birthday on 9 September 1999; to Edinburgh for the 75th anniversary of Eric Liddell winning a gold medal in the Olympic Games and the opportunity to take part in a Fun Run in the playing fields where Eric trained; to Aberfoyle for a week's holiday in a Time Share Flat. We have also been getting out and about locally, walking in the Queen Elizabeth Country Park and in the forests around etc.

We joined the local Congregational Church in Rutherglen where we were made to feel very welcome. As well as attending the morning service there, we also attend Burnside Church of Scotland for their evening service. Leslie joined the Men's Fellowship and choir in the Congregational Church and Betty has joined the women's Go Ahead Club and also the High Jinks keep fit club in the Burnside Church as well as going swimming once a week in the Rutherglen indoor pool.

We have been invited to speak at various women's meetings and in churches about the work of the hospital and we hope that through this to be able to still raise support for the hospital, which we will send from time to time. The student nurses and some of the staff have written letters with news of the hospital. It is good to have their news as we long to hear how you are all faring in the hospital. You are daily in our thoughts and prayers. We were sorry to hear that Dr Hemant had not taken up the post of Medical Superintendent. We enjoyed meeting him and his family just before we left Chickballapur. We hope and pray that a Medical Superintendent will soon be found to fill the vacancy.

We wrote to some of the volunteers and medical students who had been to Chickballapur over the years, and we had an AT HOME DAY recently when several came to bring us up to date with news of their families and themselves. We hope that others will come, and we can reminisce about their time with us and their experiences since then.

After spending time in our home and doing things for ourselves, I (Betty) felt I was ready to do something for others and get involved in some voluntary work. Some of the charity shops mentioned earlier had requests in their shops for volunteers to help in the shops so I offered myself to one, Marie Curie Cancer Care shop. I have been going there on a Friday morning and I am enjoying the experience. I am amazed at the nearly new, and sometimes really new, clothes, books, ornaments, household items, jewellery etc. handed in by people, for sale in aid of this charity. I have been able to buy some things for myself and for the house, and get good bargains. I am amazed at the good quality of things being thrown out by people but really welcomed in our shop so that the charity can benefit from the sales.

In church one Sunday volunteers were asked to help with Meals on Wheels, which is organised by the WRVS (Women's Royal Voluntary Service). I volunteered for this but have not yet been called to help. For this service, meals are prepared and kept in hot containers and delivered to the homes of elderly or handicapped people who are not able to cook a meal for themselves. The meals are subsidised but the people pay a certain amount towards the cost, and this ensures that they get a hot meal twice a week.

At all the women's meetings and other gatherings we have attended we have had the Chickballapur Christmas cards, books *Hot Surgery* and *Jackfruit and Wild Honey* for sale, as well as a supply of pens with the hospital name on them, in aid of hospital funds. I also continue to knit while watching television or while going on long-distance bus and train journeys and later will send a parcel of jumpers and cardigans, baby bonnets and bootees etc. to the hospital.

I am writing this letter on the computer, which we bought soon after we settled in. I am still getting to grips with all the intricacies and could do with a person to sit by my side to help me when I am stuck. Slowly with some help from time to time, I am learning all the marvellous things that can be done on a computer. Recently, we were connected to the Internet and email, and this is another new discovery for both of us. Now, we want to get some email addresses in India so that we can be in touch quicker and cheaper than writing letters, and sending by airmail. Last week there was a strike of post office workers and although it lasted only a few days it meant there was a pile-up of letters waiting to be delivered.

In the past, our circular letter was illustrated and sent out by our friend Grace Dunlop, but this year we are attempting to do it ourselves! We are very grateful for the many years Grace has done this for us and kept in touch with donors who have sent gifts for the hospital.

As we prepare for our first Christmas in Scotland after more than 30 in India, we send our greetings to all our friends and colleagues in India and elsewhere. We will be very much with you in spirit although not there in person. We look forward to keeping in touch and hearing from you if not meeting you in the coming year.

Betty and Leslie